Instant Apache ActiveMQ Messaging Application Development How-to

Develop message-based applications using ActiveMQ and the JMS

Timothy Bish

PUBLISHING

BIRMINGHAM - MUMBAI

Instant Apache ActiveMQ Messaging Application Development How-to

First published: May 2013

Production Reference: 1170513

Published by Packt Publishing Ltd.
Livery Place
35 Livery Street
Birmingham B3 2PB, UK.

ISBN 978-1-78216-941-3

www.packtpub.com

Credits

Author
Timothy Bish

Reviewers
Rob Davies
Christian Posta

Acquisition Editors
Andrew Duckworth
Rubal Kaur

Commissioning Editor
Yogesh Dalvi

Technical Editors
Rutvij Karkhanis
Pushpak Poddar
Varun Pius Rodrigues

Copy Editors
Brandt D'Mello
Laxmi Subramanian

Project Coordinator
Esha Thakker

Proofreader
Kevin McGowan

Graphics
Abhinash Sahu

Production Coordinator
Nitesh Thakur

Cover Work
Nitesh Thakur

Cover image
Aditi Gajjar

About the Author

Timothy Bish is a senior software engineer currently working for RedHat Inc. He currently works out of his home in Alexandria, VA, actively contributing to the ActiveMQ Project. Timothy started his work in the open source world as a side project while working for a company in Syracuse NY. What started as something fun turned into a full time career and remains a passion for Timothy.

Timothy started his career in software development in 1999 and has worked for several years in the private sector before moving into full time open source development. During that time Timothy earned his Masters of Computer Engineering from Syracuse University. Having worked on a number of home grown Messaging frameworks Timothy has seen firsthand how the world of open source software like ActiveMQ has transformed the development world.

Besides working on new development projects Timothy also enjoys reading, skiing, scuba diving, and traveling to new and exotic places.

I'd like to thank my wife for all her support and encouragement while I worked on this book. I'd also like to thank my good friend Nate for sending me down a road to what has become a fun and exciting career.

About the Reviewer

Rob Davies is the technical director for Fuse Engineering at Red Hat. Previously, Rob was the CTO of FuseSource—the experts in open source integration and messaging. With 20 years experience of architecting solutions and developing products for large-scale distributed applications for telcos and finance, Rob is focusing on developing the next generation of open source middleware products for Red Hat.

Rob's first experience in startups was WatchMark, which span out of US-West and Cable and Wireless. Subsequently, Rob co-founded SpiritSoft, where he was initially CEO, then CTO, and helped raise $20 million in venture capital. SpiritSoft, specialising in middleware products for finance, was acquired by Seebeyond in 2005. Rob went on to co-found LogicBlaze, a Los Angeles based startup that created open source integration and messaging middleware, and which was sold to IONA Technologies in 2007.

Rob was the co-founder and contributor to Apache ActiveMQ, ServiceMix, and Camel.

Christian Posta, based in Phoenix, AZ, is a senior consultant and architect and specializes in messaging-based enterprise integrations. He has been developing for over 10 years doing a wide range of stuff from embedded systems to UI and UX design and lots of integration in between. He's passionate about software development, loves solving tough technical problems, and enjoys learning new languages and programming paradigms. His favorite languages include Python and Scala, but he spends a lot of time writing Java. He is a committer on Apache ActiveMQ and Apache Apollo projects and frequently blogs at http://www.christianposta.com/blog as well as tweeting about interesting technology @christianposta.

Thanks to Timothy and Packt for asking me to review the book. I think it will be very useful for those getting into messaging and ActiveMQ specifically. There's a lot to learn, but this book takes a step-by-step approach to clearly present the road to take for understanding the concepts.

www.PacktPub.com

Support files, eBooks, discount offers and more

You might want to visit www.PacktPub.com for support files and downloads related to your book.

Did you know that Packt offers eBook versions of every book published, with PDF and ePub files available? You can upgrade to the eBook version at www.PacktPub.com and as a print book customer, you are entitled to a discount on the eBook copy. Get in touch with us at service@packtpub.com for more details.

At www.PacktPub.com, you can also read a collection of free technical articles, sign up for a range of free newsletters and receive exclusive discounts and offers on Packt books and eBooks.

http://PacktLib.PacktPub.com

Do you need instant solutions to your IT questions? PacktLib is Packt's online digital book library. Here, you can access, read and search across Packt's entire library of books.

Why Subscribe?

- ► Fully searchable across every book published by Packt
- ► Copy and paste, print and bookmark content
- ► On demand and accessible via web browser

Free Access for Packt account holders

If you have an account with Packt at www.PacktPub.com, you can use this to access PacktLib today and view nine entirely free books. Simply use your login credentials for immediate access.

Table of Contents

Preface   **1**

Instant Apache ActiveMQ Messaging Application Development How-to   **7**

Installing ActiveMQ (Simple)   7
Setting up our development environment (Simple)   10
Creating ActiveMQ applications (Simple)   12
Dividing up work with queues (Simple)   18
Event processing with topics (Simple)   24
Selecting messages (Simple)   30
Using the JMS request/response pattern (Intermediate)   34
Scheduling message delivery (Advanced)   40
Activity monitoring in ActiveMQ (Advanced)   46
Application testing using embedded brokers (Advanced)   50
Using ActiveMQ connection pools (Advanced)   54
Using Virtual Destinations (Advanced)   59
Using Failover transport (Advanced)   62

Preface

The problem of transferring data from one application to another one is not new. Ever since the advent of computer networks, developers have had to create solutions for this problem, which have evolved into their own engineering domain—Enterprise Messaging. The applications that operate in this domain have come to be known as message-oriented middleware (MOM).

In the early days, MOM solutions were closed-source applications that relied on proprietary protocols and had no standardized API for developers to use. This led to software that was locked into the MOM provider that was originally chosen, and switching to an alternative MOM provider was a difficult if not insurmountable process.

ActiveMQ is an open source MOM application used around the world in enterprise and academic projects. ActiveMQ provides a wealth of features and can be accessed from clients written in languages such as Java, C, C++, .NET, and Python.

Because of the vast array of features that ActiveMQ supports, getting started with developing applications for it can be quite daunting. In this book we will learn how to get started with writing applications that leverage ActiveMQ. We will start out with the basics of writing JMS-based applications and then learn how to leverage some of ActiveMQ's more advanced features to supercharge our applications.

What this book covers

Installing ActiveMQ (Simple) provides a brief walkthrough of the steps necessary to download and install Apache ActiveMQ v5.8.0 and get it running.

Setting up our development environment (Simple) has a brief look at the steps necessary to set up an environment for building and running the examples in this book.

Creating ActiveMQ applications (Simple) shows how to create a simple ActiveMQ application that can send and receive a message. We cover all the steps needed to write the code, build, and run the application.

Dividing up work with queues (Simple) explores how to spread out the work of processing jobs using JMS queues. We examine the properties of a JMS queue and learn how to leverage them to balance the load among many queue consumers.

Event processing with topics (Simple) explores JMS topics and how the properties of the publish/subscribe destinations allow us to send events to our JMS applications.

Selecting messages (Simple) explores the JMS message selector and how it can be used to instruct ActiveMQ about which messages our consumers are really interested in receiving.

Using the JMS request/response pattern (Intermediate) looks at how we can implement applications that send out requests over JMS queues and wait for responses to our requests.

Scheduling message delivery (Advanced) explores the capability of ActiveMQ to schedule messages for delivery at a later date.

Activity monitoring in ActiveMQ (Advanced) shows us how to listen in on any activity that's occurring on an ActiveMQ broker using its built-in advisory topics.

Application testing using embedded brokers (Advanced) shows us how to leverage ActiveMQ's ability to be embedded into any Java application, to test our messaging applications.

Using ActiveMQ connection pools (Advanced) explores the features of the connection pooling library provided by ActiveMQ to improve the performance of our applications and also looks at why pooling is not always the right answer.

Using Virtual Destinations (Advanced) shows us an advanced feature in ActiveMQ called Virtual Destinations, and how we can use it to overcome the limitations of JMS's durable topic subscriptions.

Using Failover transport (Advanced) shows us how to improve the reliability of our applications by using ActiveMQ's Failover transport in our clients, to automatically reconnect to a broker when our connection is lost.

What you need for this book

In order to build and run the examples that accompany this book, you will need an installation of Java 1.6 or later, Apache Maven 3.0.2 or higher, and a copy of Apache ActiveMQ v5.8.0.

Who this book is for

This book is targeted at the Java developer who might be new to message-orientated middleware and specifically the JMS specification and its use in the development of applications that use ActiveMQ or other JMS-compliant messaging brokers.

Conventions

In this book, you will find a number of styles of text that distinguish between different kinds of information. Here are some examples of these styles, and an explanation of their meaning.

Code words in text are shown as follows: " You can start the broker now assuming your Java installation is correct by running the `activemq` script"

A block of code is set as follows:

```
Class MyTransportListener implements TransportListener {
    public void onCommand(Object command) {}

    public void onException(IOException error) {

    public void transportInterupted() {
        // app logic
    }

    public void transportResumed() {
        // app logic
    }
}


    MyTransportListener listener = new MyTransportListener();
    ((ActiveMQConnection) connection).addTransportListener(listener);
```

When we wish to draw your attention to a particular part of a code block, the relevant lines or items are set in bold:

```
    public void run() throws Exception {
        MessageProducer producer =
            session.createProducer(destination);

        for (int i = 0; i < 1000; ++i) {
            TextMessage message =
                session.createTextMessage(
                    "Job number: " + i);
            message.setIntProperty("JobID", i);
            producer.send(message);
        }

        producer.close();
    }
```

Any command-line input or output is written as follows:

```
:~$ java -version
java version "1.6.0_41"
Java(TM) SE Runtime Environment (build 1.6.0_41-b02-445-11M4107)
Java HotSpot(TM) 64-Bit Server VM (build 20.14-b01-445, mixed mode)
```

New terms and **important words** are shown in bold. Words that you see on the screen, in menus or dialog boxes for example, appear in the text like this: "clicking the **Next** button moves you to the next screen".

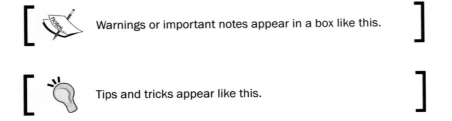

Warnings or important notes appear in a box like this.

Tips and tricks appear like this.

Reader feedback

Feedback from our readers is always welcome. Let us know what you think about this book—what you liked or may have disliked. Reader feedback is important for us to develop titles that you really get the most out of.

To send us general feedback, simply send an e-mail to feedback@packtpub.com, and mention the book title via the subject of your message.

If there is a topic that you have expertise in and you are interested in either writing or contributing to a book, see our author guide on www.packtpub.com/authors.

Customer support

Now that you are the proud owner of a Packt book, we have a number of things to help you to get the most from your purchase.

Downloading the example code

You can download the example code files for all Packt books you have purchased from your account at http://www.packtpub.com. If you purchased this book elsewhere, you can visit http://www.packtpub.com/support and register to have the files e-mailed directly to you.

Errata

Although we have taken every care to ensure the accuracy of our content, mistakes do happen. If you find a mistake in one of our books—maybe a mistake in the text or the code—we would be grateful if you would report this to us. By doing so, you can save other readers from frustration and help us improve subsequent versions of this book. If you find any errata, please report them by visiting http://www.packtpub.com/submit-errata, selecting your book, clicking on the **errata submission form** link, and entering the details of your errata. Once your errata are verified, your submission will be accepted and the errata will be uploaded on our website, or added to any list of existing errata, under the Errata section of that title. Any existing errata can be viewed by selecting your title from http://www.packtpub.com/support.

Piracy

Piracy of copyright material on the Internet is an ongoing problem across all media. At Packt, we take the protection of our copyright and licenses very seriously. If you come across any illegal copies of our works, in any form, on the Internet, please provide us with the location address or website name immediately so that we can pursue a remedy.

Please contact us at copyright@packtpub.com with a link to the suspected pirated material.

We appreciate your help in protecting our authors, and our ability to bring you valuable content.

Questions

You can contact us at questions@packtpub.com if you are having a problem with any aspect of the book, and we will do our best to address it.

Instant Apache ActiveMQ Messaging Application Development How-to

At its core ActiveMQ is a **Java Messaging Service** (**JMS**) specification-compliant **Message-oriented middleware** (**MOM**) broker. In this book we are going to explore the JMS application development model using ActiveMQ. We will also look at some features of ActiveMQ that go beyond what's provided in the plain JMS specification.

Installing ActiveMQ (Simple)

Before you can start developing with ActiveMQ you need to install the ActiveMQ Broker and get it running on your system. We'll cover the basic steps needed to install ActiveMQ here.

Getting ready

The first thing you need to do is ensure that you have the Java SDK installed. ActiveMQ v5.8.0 requires at least Java 1.6, although 1.7 is also supported. If your computer doesn't already have the Java SDK installed, you need to download a version appropriate for your operating system before we can continue. You can get the latest version from `http://www.oracle.com/technetwork/java/javase/downloads/index.html`.

While you're downloading that, you can go and download the latest version of ActiveMQ as well. ActiveMQ comes in either a `tar.gz` or ZIP archive and the version we will be using in this book (5.8.0) is available at `http://activemq.apache.org/activemq-580-release.html`.

How to do it...

Follow the installation instructions on the J2SE site if you need to install Java on your system. Once you're ready, you can test out your installation of Java from an open terminal; your output should look something like this:

```
:~$ java -version
java version "1.6.0_41"
Java(TM) SE Runtime Environment (build 1.6.0_41-b02-445-11M4107)
Java HotSpot(TM) 64-Bit Server VM (build 20.14-b01-445, mixed mode)
```

Now that you have a working Java installation, you can move on to installing ActiveMQ on your system by following these simple steps:

1. Extract the ActiveMQ archive you downloaded to a permanent location on your computer.

2. Next, open a terminal and change to the directory where you extracted the ActiveMQ archive.

3. You can start the broker now, assuming your Java installation is correct, by running the `activemq` script located in the `bin` directory, your terminal should look something like the following console output:

```
$./bin/activemq start
INFO: Using default configuration

INFO: Invoke the following command to create a configuration file
./bin/activemq setup

INFO: Starting - inspect logfiles specified in logging.properties
and log4j.properties to get details
INFO: pidfile created : '
(pid '9324')
```

When started in this manner, the broker runs as a background process; to stop the broker you issue the following command in the same terminal window:

```
$./bin/activemq stop


INFO: Invoke the following command to create a configuration file
./bin/activemq setup


INFO: Waiting at least 30 seconds for regular process termination
of pid '9640' :
Java Runtime: Apple Inc. 1.6.0_41
   Heap sizes: current=1035520k  free=1033420k  max=1035520k
     JVM args: -Xms1G -Xmx1G -
Connecting to pid: 9640
Stopping broker: localhost
... FINISHED
```

Congratulations! You've installed ActiveMQ and are ready to move on to setting up your development environment and writing your first ActiveMQ applications.

There's more...

Your ActiveMQ installation is shipped with a set of default configuration files that provide a basic broker configuration adequate for testing. In production environments, you will find you need to tweak many of the settings to get the most out of your ActiveMQ Broker. Refer to the ActiveMQ website for more information on the various configuration options that are available. You can find the broker configuration in the directory named conf in your installation directory. You can easily start up an instance of ActiveMQ using one of the sample configurations on the command line by passing in the file you want to use as follows:

```
$./bin/activemq start xbean:./conf/activemq-stomp.xml
```

When changing configuration options it's a good idea to start up your broker in foreground mode to verify that your changes didn't break anything. You start the broker in foreground mode by entering the following into the terminal once you change the directory to the location in which you installed ActiveMQ:

```
$./bin/activemq console
```

Your broker will start up and display a large amount of configuration information as its starting point and will display error information if it encounters any. To stop your broker when it is running in foreground mode simply press *Ctrl + C*. You can also use the activemq. log file located in the data directory to check for errors after you've started the broker.

Setting up our development environment (Simple)

Now that we have a broker installed and know how to start and stop it, we need to gather together the tools we will need to craft our ActiveMQ applications.

We will be using Apache Maven throughout this book to build and run the examples. Maven is a build management tool that provides a simple way to create Java applications using an XML-based project file called a POM file. You can learn more about Maven by visiting the project website at `http://maven.apache.org/index.html`.

Getting ready

In order to install Apache Maven, you need to download it from the Maven download page located here: `http://maven.apache.org/download.cgi`

How to do it...

You install Maven by following these steps:

1. Download and extract the Maven distribution appropriate for your OS into a permanent location.
2. Create an environment variable called `M2_HOME` that references the installation directory you chose in Step 1.
3. Add the Maven executable to your system path using the `M2_HOME/bin` location.

You should now be able to check on your Maven installation by opening a terminal and executing the following:

```
$ mvn -version
Apache Maven 3.0.3 (r1075438; 2011-02-28 12:31:09-0500)
Maven home: /usr/share/maven
Java version: 1.6.0_41, vendor: Apple Inc.

Default locale: en_US, platform encoding: MacRoman
OS name: "mac os x", version: "10.8.2", arch: "x86_64", family: "mac"
```

You should see output that looks similar to the preceding code. If you don't, you should refer to the Maven instructions instruction located on the download page at `http://maven.apache.org/download.cgi`.

How it works...

Apache Maven organizes your code into projects that are configured and managed using an XML file named `pom.xml`. The examples for each recipe in this book are separated into individual Maven projects that make it simple for you to build and run the code without having to set up your own builds.

 Keep in mind that Maven requires an Internet connection in order to download the plugins and project dependencies for you from the Maven site. Once you've built and installed the project in your local Maven repo, you can go offline if you need to and still run the project.

Now that you have Maven installed and working, it's a good idea to try and build the samples that we will be using throughout this book to ensure that everything is working as expected and to gain some experience building a Maven project.

Assuming you've already downloaded and extracted the source archive for the sample ActiveMQ applications, open a terminal and change to the samples directory. In the terminal, enter the following command:

```
$mvn compile
```

After running this command you'll most likely see a lot of information flowing by in the terminal as Maven downloads the various dependencies for the projects and runs the builds for each. At the end of the build process you should see a message informing you that the build was successful, a truncated sample is shown in the following code:

```
[INFO] --------------------------------------------------------------
[INFO] Building ActiveMQ-Application-Development-Examples 1.0
[INFO] --------------------------------------------------------------
[INFO] --------------------------------------------------------------
[INFO] Reactor Summary:
[INFO]
[INFO] Simple-JMS-Application ......................... SUCCESS [0.630s]
[INFO] JobProducer ................................... SUCCESS [0.014s]
[INFO] JobConsumer ................................... SUCCESS [0.013s]
[INFO] ActiveMQ-Application-Development-Examples ...... SUCCESS [0.000s]
```

```
[INFO] ------------------------------------------------------------------------
[INFO] BUILD SUCCESS
[INFO] ------------------------------------------------------------------------
[INFO] Total time: 0.780s
[INFO] Finished at: Sun Feb 24 17:37:11 EST 2013
[INFO] Final Memory: 4M/265M
[INFO] ------------------------------------------------------------------------
```

If you don't see a `BUILD SUCCESS` in your own build, something went wrong and you may need to refer to the troubleshooting information on the Maven website.

There's more...

If you are more comfortable working with code in an **integrated development environment** (**IDE**), it's quite simple to use the provided sample applications from most IDEs as long as they have support for Maven projects. Most modern IDEs have built in support for Maven projects and you simply need to import the project into the IDE by following the instructions provided by the IDE documentation. There are many freely available IDEs to choose from if you don't already have one installed; Eclipse is a good choice since it's free, IntelliJ also comes in a free community edition and integrates well with Maven projects.

Creating ActiveMQ applications (Simple)

In this recipe we are going to create a very simple JMS application that places a message on a queue in ActiveMQ and consumes that message from the queue immediately after. This example demonstrates many of the JMS APIs that we will be using in the future recipes.

Getting ready

In this recipe, we will be referencing the `simple-jms-application` project that contains the full working code and Maven POM file. You should have a default installation of the ActiveMQ Broker running before attempting to execute the sample application in this recipe.

How to do it...

To run the sample for this recipe you will need to perform the following steps:

1. Open a terminal and start an instance of the ActiveMQ Broker.
2. Open a second command-line window, change to the directory where the `simple-jms-application` project is located, and execute the following command:

```
mvn compile exec:java
```

This will build and run the sample application and you should see an output similar to the following, assuming everything goes well:

```
INFO] Scanning for projects...
[INFO]
[INFO] ------------------------------------------------------------------------
[INFO] Building Simple-JMS-Application 1.0
[INFO] ------------------------------------------------------------------------
[INFO]


Starting SimpleJMS example now...
Producer sent a Message
Consumer received a Message, it reads: Woohoo!
Finished running the SimpleJMS example.


[INFO] ------------------------------------------------------------------------
[INFO] BUILD SUCCESS
[INFO] ------------------------------------------------------------------------
[INFO] Total time: 1.249s
[INFO] Finished at: Mon Feb 25 17:19:30 EST 2013
[INFO] Final Memory: 6M/265M
[INFO] ------------------------------------------------------------------------
```

How it works...

Now that we've run the example, let's take a look at the code and see how it works. The complete source code is located in the file `SimpleJMS.java` in the example `simple-jms-application`. You are encouraged to open the file and refer to it during this discussion.

This example defines three methods: `before()`, `run()`, and `after()`, which we call in sequence. Each of these methods breaks out the basic steps you must do in any JMS application:

```
public class SimpleJMS {

    private final String connectionUri = "tcp://localhost:61616";
    private ActiveMQConnectionFactory connectionFactory;
    private Connection connection;
    private Session session;
    private Destination destination;

    public void before() throws Exception {
        connectionFactory = new
            ActiveMQConnectionFactory(connectionUri);
        connection = connectionFactory.createConnection();
        connection.start();
        session = connection.createSession(
            false, Session.AUTO_ACKNOWLEDGE);
        destination = session.createQueue("MyQueue");
    }
```

In the `before()` method we set up our connection to the ActiveMQ Broker and create the basic JMS boilerplate objects that we'll use in the `run()` method later. The setup here proceeds as follows:

1. Create a new JMS `ConnectionFactory` using the concrete type `ActiveMQConnectionFactory`, which is provided in the ActiveMQ client library. The `ConnectionFactory` is supplied the URI of our running broker, namely, `tcp://localhost:61616`. Every `ActiveMQConnectionFactory` needs a URI telling where and how to connect to the broker.

2. Create a new JMS `Connection` object by invoking the `ConnectionFactory` object's `createConnection` method. If the connection to the broker cannot be created we will get an exception at this point.

3. We can now start our new `Connection`. A JMS `Connection` object won't deliver any messages to your `MessageConsumer` until you start it so it's very important to remember to call `connection.start()`.

4. Create a new JMS `Session` object by calling the `Connection` object's `createSession()` method. Since `Session` requires a message acknowledgement mode, we specify that in the `createSession()` method. We choose auto acknowledgement mode so we don't have to worry about manually acknowledging messages in this simple application.

5. Finally we create a `Destination` object that our application's `producer` and `consumer` will use to send and receive our simple message. In our example we create a queue but it would work exactly the same if we had used a Topic domain for this simple example.

Once the `before()` method completes, our little application is ready to go; so we next call the `run()` method to do the work. The code for the `run()` method is shown next:

Downloading the example code

You can download the example code files for all Packt books you have purchased from your account at http://www.packtpub.com. If you purchased this book elsewhere, you can visit http://www.packtpub.com/support and register to have the files e-mailed directly to you.

```java
public void run() throws Exception {
    MessageProducer producer =
        session.createProducer(destination);
    try {
        TextMessage message = session.createTextMessage();
        message.setText("Woohoo!");
        producer.send(message);
    } finally {
        producer.close();
    }

    MessageConsumer consumer =
        session.createConsumer(destination);
    try {
        TextMessage message =
            (TextMessage) consumer.receive();
    } finally {
        consumer.close();
    }
}
```

This method is divided into two parts, one of which performs the send of our simple message and then our attempts to receive it. Let's break down the send portion first:

1. Using the `Session` we created earlier, we first create a `MessageProducer`; this is the object that will allow us to send our simple message.

2. Create a new `TextMessage` object using the `Session` object and assign it a payload at the same time.

3. Send the message using the `MessageProducer` object's `send()` method. The `MessageProducer` object knows where to send the message since we passed in a `Destination` object when we created it.

4. Finally, we close down the `MessageProducer` object since we won't use it again in this application.

Now that we've seen how a message is sent, we can look at how receiver code works:

1. First we create a `MessageConsumer` object using `Session` just as we did for the `MessageProducer` previously

2. We use the `MessageConsumer` object blocking the `receive()` call to wait for the broker to route the message we sent previously to our producer

3. Once we receive the message we need to cast it to the correct type since the `receive()` method returns a base message reference

4. We print out a little message showing the payload of the `TextMessage` we sent previously

5. Finally, we close down our consumer since we are done with that as well

All that's left is to call the `after()` method, which simply closes the `Connection` object we opened in the `before()` method and our application comes to an end.

```
public void after() throws Exception {
    if (connection != null) {
        connection.close();
    }
}
```

Closing `Connection` will take care of closing out any resources created by the connection, so we omit the call to the `close()` method of our `Session`.

This simple application demonstrates many of the elements of the JMS API that you will use in the messaging applications that you write in the future. Unlike our future examples this one incorporates both a producer and consumer within the same application. In our future examples, we will generally break apart the producer and consumer into separate applications for a more realistic demonstration.

There's more...

Before we move onto the remainder of the examples in this book, it's a good idea to understand the Maven project files that build and run our projects. A Maven POM file defines the various modules of a project and allows us to specify all the required libraries we need to be assembled in order for our project to run. Maven also allows for various plugins to be specified in the POM file that can perform actions beyond just compiling code and downloading dependencies. Let's take a look at the POM file that we used to run our first application, it's located in the directory of our `simple-jms-application` example:

```xml
<project xmlns="http://maven.apache.org/POM/4.0.0" xmlns:xsi="http://
www.w3.org/2001/XMLSchema-instance" xsi:schemaLocation="http://maven.
apache.org/POM/4.0.0 http://maven.apache.org/xsd/maven-4.0.0.xsd">

    <modelVersion>4.0.0</modelVersion>
    <groupId>org.apache.activemq.recipes</groupId>
    <artifactId>SimpleJMS</artifactId>
    <version>1.0</version>
    <name>Simple-JMS-Application</name>
    <description>A simple JMS application</description>

    <dependencies>
      <dependency>
        <groupId>org.apache.activemq</groupId>
        <artifactId>activemq-client</artifactId>
        <version>5.8.0</version>
      </dependency>
      <dependency>
        <groupId>org.slf4j</groupId>
        <artifactId>slf4j-log4j12</artifactId>
        <version>1.7.2</version>
      </dependency>
    </dependencies>

</project>
```

As you can see, the POM file is just a basic XML file with sections for project dependencies and a section for specifying the plugins used in the build process.

Take note of the dependencies that we specified in our SimpleJMS application's POM file. We only needed to bring in the `<activemq-client>` dependency and a log4j plugin so that the ActiveMQ client knows what logger our project is using. Maven figures everything else out for us so that we don't have to fuss with classpath issues and just focus on our ActiveMQ skills. It's good to get an idea of how Maven works if you haven't used it already as it can greatly streamline your build process.

A brief aside on Connection URIs

In our SimpleJMS application we created a connection to the ActiveMQ Broker by creating an instance of `ActiveMQConnectionFactory` and giving it a URI string that told it how to connect to ActiveMQ. We used the string, `tcp://localhost:61616` in our example, which tells the client that it should use a TCP-style connection to connect to the broker on port 61616. ActiveMQ supports a number of different connection options beyond TCP such as SSL, HTTP, NIO, and more. You can get more information on how to use those connection types and on configuration options that can be added to the URI string on the ActiveMQ website, the following links provide an overview of the connection URI configuration syntax and options:

- `http://activemq.apache.org/configuring-transports.html`
- `http://activemq.apache.org/connection-configuration-uri.html`

Dividing up work with queues (Simple)

In this recipe we look at how the JMS queue can be used to divide up work with a simple job queue example.

Getting ready

For this recipe we will use the two examples named `job-producer` and `job-consumer` that implement a simple job producer and consumer.

How to do it...

To run the sample for this recipe you will need to perform the following steps:

1. Open a terminal and start a broker.

2. Open a second terminal and change to the directory where `job-consumer` is located. Run the consumer by typing `mvn compile exec:java`. (You can use *Ctrl + C* to terminate this app when done, it will stop on its own after five minutes.)

3. Open a third terminal and change to the directory where `job-producer` is located and run the producer by typing `mvn compile exec:java`.

In the terminal where you started the job producer you will see an output like the following indicating that the producer is queuing up work for our consumer:

```
Starting example Job Q Producer now...
Producer sent Job(0)
Producer sent Job(1)
Producer sent Job(2)
Producer sent Job(3)
Producer sent Job(4)
```

And in the terminal where you started the consumer you should see that the consumer is consuming the jobs as they are placed into the queue:

```
Starting example Job Consumer now...
Worker processing job: 0
Worker processing job: 1
Worker processing job: 2
Worker processing job: 3
Worker processing job: 4
```

How it works...

As your producer and consumer runs, you will see output in the terminal windows showing the producer placing jobs onto the JMS queue and the consumer removing a job from the queue and log it has just completed. You could also start up yet another consumer instance in another terminal and the jobs would be divided between each running consumer.

A JMS queue represents a type of messaging domain known as point-to-point messaging. When a message is sent to a queue and subsequently dispatched to a consumer it's sent only to that consumer and no other. This type of message dispatching is often referred to as "once and only once dispatch".

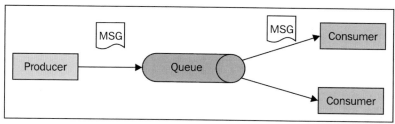

JMS queue domains

In the preceding figure we see a fairly typical queue scenario in which we have one producer sending a message to our queue, and there are two consumers who are interested in receiving messages that are placed in the queue. When the JMS provider dispatches the queued message, it will pick one of the consumers and send that message only to that consumer; generally the second consumer would receive the next message placed on the queue, as distribution tends to be round robin.

What would happen if our producer sent a message and there were no consumers to receive it? In that case the queue would hold onto the message until a consumer arrived to dequeue it, or if it has a set expiration it will be removed once that time has elapsed.

The properties of the JMS queue make it an ideal means of processing jobs; let's review those properties again in the context of a job processing application:

- Messages placed on a queue are persisted until they are consumed by `MessageConsumer`, jobs aren't lost if no active consumer is online.

- Queued messages can have a **time to live** (**TTL**) set, which causes them to time out and be removed from the queue. This is good if a queued job is time sensitive.

- Queued messages are delivered in the order they were placed on the queue if a single consumer is active, this is good if the jobs are order dependent.

- When more than one consumer is reading from the queue, the messages on the queue are spread out among all active consumers to allow for load balancing of your queued up jobs.

Now, let's take a look at the job producer applications, then we'll explore job consumer in depth.

The job producer

The code for the job queue producer looks a lot like the code we saw in our first recipe, the SimpleJMS application. We see some minor changes to remove the consumer and add in the code to produce a series of jobs to our queue:

```
public class JobProducer {

    private final String connectionUri = "tcp://localhost:61616";
    private ActiveMQConnectionFactory connectionFactory;
    private Connection connection;
    private Session session;
    private Destination destination;

    public void before() throws Exception {
        connectionFactory = new
            ActiveMQConnectionFactory(connectionUri);
```

```
        connection = connectionFactory.createConnection();
        session = connection.createSession(
            false, Session.AUTO_ACKNOWLEDGE);
        destination = session.createQueue("JOBQ.Work");
    }

    public void run() throws Exception {
        MessageProducer producer =
            session.createProducer(destination);

        for (int i = 0; i < 1000; ++i) {
            TextMessage message =
                session.createTextMessage(
                    "Job number: " + i);
            message.setIntProperty("JobID", i);
            producer.send(message);
        }

        producer.close();
    }
}
```

The crux of the job producer lies in the `for` loop in the `run()` method, here we create a series of 1,000 `TextMessage` objects and assign each a unique identifier and a simple message body. Of course in a real application the type of message we send can be any of the JMS message types and the payload of the message would most likely be much more substantial, for example, an XML file containing a product ordered from an online retailer. The point to keep in mind here is that our job producer doesn't need to know anything about the consumers it just happily sends out the work and trusts that someone will take it from there. Let's move on then to the job consumer code.

The job consumer

The code for the job consumer is shown next. You should again notice that the job consumer code looks much like our SimpleJMS examples from the last recipe, which is a benefit of using a standardized API like JMS:

```
public class JobQConsumer {

    private final String connectionUri = "tcp://localhost:61616?jms.
prefetchPolicy.queuePrefetch=1";
    private ActiveMQConnectionFactory connectionFactory;
    private Connection connection;
    private Session session;
```

```
        private Destination destination;

        public void before() throws Exception {
            connectionFactory = new
                ActiveMQConnectionFactory(connectionUri);
            connection = connectionFactory.createConnection();
            connection.start();
            session = connection.createSession(
                false, Session.AUTO_ACKNOWLEDGE);
            destination = session.createQueue("JOBQ.Work");
        }

        public void run() throws Exception {
            MessageConsumer consumer =
                session.createConsumer(destination);
            consumer.setMessageListener(new JobQListener());
            TimeUnit.MINUTES.sleep(5);
            connection.stop();
            consumer.close();
        }
    }
```

Most of the code here isn't really new, however, the job consumer code does introduce some JMS API usage we've not seen before, namely, an asynchronous `MessageListener` object for processing our jobs. The code for the `MessageListener` implementation is shown in full next. This is where the real work is done for our queued jobs.

```
    public class JobQListener implements MessageListener {

        private final Random jobDelay = new Random();

        public void onMessage(Message message) {
            try {
                int jobId = message.getIntProperty("JobID");
                System.out.println("Worker processing job: " + jobId);
                TimeUnit.MILLISECONDS.sleep(jobDelay.nextInt(100));
            } catch (Exception e) {
                System.out.println("Worker caught an Exception");
            }
        }
    }
```

The `MessageListener` object in JMS allows us to receive and process messages asynchronously, freeing up our application to do other work if it needs to while messages are processed in a separate thread.

You might be wondering why we didn't just use the synchronous receive methods that were used in the SimpleJMS application we looked at in the previous recipe. We very well could have written the application to call the `MessageConsumer` object's synchronous receive call, there's just a few points to keep in mind when you choose that route. When you use the synchronous receive call, the thread is blocked waiting on a message, it can't do any other work. Also when you go the synchronous route, you need to provide some means of breaking the thread out of the receive call either via timeout or by having some other thread close to the `MessageConsumer` or `Connection` object that owns it. Using the asynchronous style gives you more flexibility in your application design.

In a typical job processing application the number of jobs to process is not set. It's also common to have more than one queue that holds jobs to be processed. Because messages sent to a Queue are evenly dispatched to the `MessageConsumer` objects that have subscribed to it, we can easily deal with increasing numbers of messages by adding more consumer applications to process them if the current consumers become overloaded.

There's more...

When working with JMS queues and ActiveMQ, it's good to understand the idea of **message prefetching**. ActiveMQ will send a set number of messages to a new consumer when it subscribes to a destination if that destination has pending messages. The number of messages sent is known as the consumer's prefetch limit; the default prefetch limit for a queue, for instance, is 1,000 messages.

Why is this prefetch limit thing important? For a single consumer on a destination, prefetching the messages can speed up message processing since there will always be messages waiting on the client end of the `Connection` object as opposed to having to wait after every message acknowledgement for the broker to send across another message. When there's more than one consumer subscribed to a destination, that's when things can get interesting.

Let's say, for instance, you wanted to have two consumers processing jobs from a queue and there are 500 messages (jobs) on the queue. Depending on the time interval between consumer 1 subscribing to the queue and consumer 2 subscribing, ActiveMQ could have sent all 500 Messages to the first consumer since its default prefetch size is 1,000. This is not ideal as consumer 2 now sits idle and consumer 1 must process all 500 jobs on its own, so your consumers won't do any load balancing. It's important when you are designing your queue processing applications then to tune the prefetch value for your consumers in order to get the behavior and performance characteristics desired.

In our sample job consumer application, we actually did do this; were you paying attention? Take another look at the `Connection` URI used in the sample:

```
private final String connectionUri = "tcp://localhost:61616?jms.
prefetchPolicy.queuePrefetch=1";
```

The addition to the prefetch policy setting for queues of 1 means that ActiveMQ will only send one message to our application and won't send another until the `onMessage` call of our `MessageListener` returns and the message is acknowledged. You can observe the effects that changing the prefetch will have by changing the value used in the application to something like 500 or 1,000.

You should try changing this value and running several instances of the job consumer application to see the effect of this setting on them. You can read more about prefetch configuration in ActiveMQ at `http://activemq.apache.org/what-is-the-prefetch-limit-for.html`.

Where to learn more about Message Acknowledgement

We aren't going to spend a lot of time in this book talking about the mechanics of message acknowledgement in JMS, however, this is a concept you should look into more as you become more comfortable with JMS. Refer to the JMS API documentation for some additional information on the acknowledgement modes available. Depending on your application, using acknowledgement modes other than the standard auto acknowledge mode can make a lot of sense (`http://docs.oracle.com/javaee/5/api/javax/jms/Session.html`).

Event processing with topics (Simple)

In this recipe we will explore how to use JMS topics as event channels by looking at a sample stock price update service and a simple consumer of those events.

Getting ready

For this recipe we will use the examples named `event-publisher` and `event-subscriber` that implement a simple stock price ticker application.

How to do it...

To run the sample for this recipe you will need to perform the following steps:

1. Open a terminal and start a broker.
2. Open two more terminals, change to the directory where the `event-subscriber` file is located in each, and run the consumer by typing `mvn compile exec:java`. (You can use *Ctrl + C* to terminate this application or it will stop on its own after five minutes.)

3. Open a fourth terminal, change to the directory where the `event-publisher` file is located, and run the producer by typing `mvn compile exec:java`.

In the terminal where you started the producer, you will see an output like the following code snippet indicating that the producer is sending events that our consumers are interested in:

```
Starting example Stock Ticker Producer now...
Producer sending price update(0)
AAPL: $ (113.95001)
GOOG: $ (645.9444)
MSFT: $ (514.129)
ORCL: $ (469.03384)
Producer sending price update(1)
AAPL: $ (163.04951)
GOOG: $ (560.21594)
```

And in the terminal windows where you started the consumers you should see that each consumer is receiving the stock price update events our producer is firing:

```
Starting example Stock Ticker Consumer now...
Price Update: AAPL[$160.8296]
Price Update: GOOG[$330.88095]
Price Update: MSFT[$301.13727]
Price Update: ORCL[$533.9956]
Price Update: AAPL[$591.5656]
Price Update: GOOG[$873.3398]
```

How it works...

This example leverages the JMS topic to send stock price updates to interested clients. A JMS topic represents a type of message domain known as **publish-subscribe messaging**. This domain differs from point-to-point messaging in two key ways. First, the messages sent to a topic are only dispatched to consumers that were listening before the message was sent. Second, every consumer listening on a topic will get a copy of the messages sent to a topic.

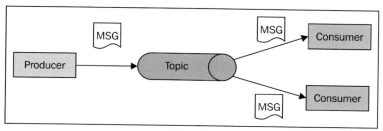

JMS topics

In the preceding figure we can see the typical JMS topic usage scenario. We have a single producer that's sending messages to a particular topic. There are two consumers that are interested in receiving messages sent to the topic and as our producer sends its messages the JMS provider dispatches a copy of the message to each consumer. If the producer were to send its messages to the topic and neither of our subscribers were currently registered, the JMS provider would simply discard those messages.

The JMS topic is ideal when you want to send notifications to clients but it's not essential that offline clients be able to consume that data when they come online again. Our stock ticker application is a good example of a use case for such a messaging domain. The client has no need for the old stock prices it only cares about the present pricing data.

Our simple stock ticker producer publishes a series of price updates for a set of stock ticker symbols to a JMS topic every five seconds. Each stock ticker consumer that we run will receive the same price update messages as they are produced. If, however, we run the price update producer to completion and then start our consumer, they would not receive any data since the JMS topic domain doesn't retain messages by default when there are no consumers.

Let's take a look at the producer and consumer applications now and see how the JMS topic messaging domain works in practice.

The stock price producer

The code for our simple stock price update producer is shown next, as you review the code take note of how much it looks like the producer from the previous recipe:

```
public class TickerProducer {

    private final String connectionUri = "tcp://localhost:61616";
    private ActiveMQConnectionFactory connectionFactory;
    private Connection connection;
    private Session session;
    private Destination destination;

    private final Random pricePicker = new Random();
    private final ArrayList<String> symbols = new
ArrayList<String>(3);

    public void before() throws Exception {
        connectionFactory = new
            ActiveMQConnectionFactory(connectionUri);
        connection = connectionFactory.createConnection();
        session = connection.createSession(
            false, Session.AUTO_ACKNOWLEDGE);
        destination = session.createTopic("EVENTS.QUOTES");
```

```
        symbols.add("AAPL"); symbols.add("GOOG");
        symbols.add("MSFT"); symbols.add("ORCL");
    }

    public void run() throws Exception {
        MessageProducer producer =
            session.createProducer(destination);

        for (int i = 0; i < 10000; ++i) {
            System.out.println("Producer sending price
update("+i+")");
            for (String symbol : symbols) {
                Message message = session.createMessage();
                message.setStringProperty("symbol", symbol);
                message.setFloatProperty(
                    "price", pricePicker.nextFloat() * 1000);
                producer.send(message);
            }
            Thread.sleep(5);
        }

        producer.close();
    }
}
```

Comparing this code to our previous queue producer code, you may have noticed that the only difference is that we created a topic destination from our session in the before() method as opposed to creating a queue destination. The JMS API makes it a simple task to transition from one messaging domain to another. If we needed our stock price updates to be preserved until some application processes each and every one of them, we could simply create a queue destination and send them there.

The stock price consumer

Our stock price update consumer is also nearly identical to the previous recipe's consumer code. The consumer code is shown next. We will follow the same model as our previous consumer by creating a class to do the JMS setup and shutdown work and then delegate the message processing to a MessageListener object.

```
public class TickerConsumer {

    private final String connectionUri = "tcp://localhost:61616";
    private ActiveMQConnectionFactory connectionFactory;
    private Connection connection;
    private Session session;
    private Destination destination;
```

```
    public void before() throws Exception {
        connectionFactory = new
            ActiveMQConnectionFactory(connectionUri);
        connection = connectionFactory.createConnection();
        connection.start();
        session = connection.createSession(
            false, Session.AUTO_ACKNOWLEDGE);
        destination = session.createTopic("EVENTS.QUOTES");
    }

    public void run() throws Exception {
        MessageConsumer consumer =
            session.createConsumer(destination);
        consumer.setMessageListener(new EventListener());
        TimeUnit.MINUTES.sleep(5);
        connection.stop();
        consumer.close();
    }
}
```

The `MessageListener` code is also just like our previous recipe's `MessageListener`; we only change what information is gathered from the message we receive. Notice that we use the simple message type as opposed to `TextMessage` since our stock pricing data is stored in the message's properties, we don't need a message body here:

```
public class EventListener implements MessageListener {
    public void onMessage(Message message) {
        try {
            float price = message.getFloatProperty("price");
            String symbol = message.getStringProperty("symbol");
        } catch (Exception e) {
        }
    }
}
```

There's more...

While it's true that the default behavior of a JMS topic is to not retain any message that is sent to it when there are no active consumers, there are cases where you might want to have a consumer go offline and, when they come back online, receive any messages that were sent while they were offline. The JMS specification provides for this by defining a type of topic subscription known as a durable subscription.

To create a durable subscription your code must call the `createDurableSubscriber()` method of a `Session` instance as well as give your connection a unique name that your application must reuse each time it runs. Let's take a look at the changes we would need to make to our stock price consumer to make it a durable subscriber:

```
public void before() throws Exception {
    connectionFactory = new
        ActiveMQConnectionFactory(connectionUri);
    connection = connectionFactory.createConnection();
    connection.setClientId("PriceConsumer");
    connection.start();
}

public void run() throws Exception {
    MessageConsumer consumer =
        session.createDurableSubscription(
            destination, "DurableConsumer");
}
```

The changes are quite minor, we simply set a client ID for our connection in the `before()` method and called durable subscription to create a method in the `run()` method. Because a durable subscription doesn't exist until it's created once, we won't see any messages if we run the consumer just once after running the stock price update producer. However, if we run the consumer once, then run the producer and the consumer a second time afterwards, we will receive all the stock price updates sent while it was offline.

Things to keep in mind when using durable subscriptions

There are several limitations that you should keep in mind when using durable subscriptions, let's take a brief look at them.

- ▸ Each JMS connection that is used to create a durable subscription must be assigned a unique client ID in order for the provider to identify the client each time its durable subscription is activated. Additionally the subscription needs its own ID value as well.

- ▸ The client must create the durable subscription at least once before the JMS provider will begin storing messages for that subscription.

- ▸ Only one JMS connection can be active at any given time for the same client ID and subscription ID meaning no load balancing is possible for multiple consumers on the same logical subscription.

These limitations make using durable subscription much more complicated than using a queue when message durability is a must. ActiveMQ provides a mechanism to help mitigate the limitations of durable subscriptions known as **Virtual Destinations**, which you should investigate any time you start to think that a durable subscription sounds like it might fit your use case. You can read about Virtual Destinations at http://activemq.apache.org/virtual-destinations.html.

In a later recipe, we will look at how we can use ActiveMQ's Virtual Destinations feature to overcome the limitations of JMS durable topic subscriptions in our applications.

Selecting messages (Simple)

Building on what we learned in the preceding recipe, we will modify our stock price consumer to use JMS selectors to filter the events it receives from the update service.

Getting ready

For this recipe we will use two examples. The first is `event-producer` that we already saw in the last recipe, and the second is `selective-event-consumer` that implements a simple stock price ticker application that uses JMS selectors to limit which stock price updates it receives.

How to do it...

To run the sample for this recipe you will need to perform the following steps:

1. Open a terminal and start a broker.
2. Open a second terminal, change to the directory where the `selective-event-consumer` file is located, and run the consumer by typing `mvn compile exec:java`. (You can use *Ctrl + C* to terminate this application or it will stop on its own after five minutes.)
3. Open a third terminal, change to the directory where `event-producer` is located, and run the producer by typing `mvn compile exec:java`.

In the terminal where you started the producer you will see an output like the following code snippet, indicating that the producer is sending events that our consumer is interested in:

```
Starting example Stock Ticker Producer now...
Producer sending price update(0)
AAPL: $ (113.95001)
GOOG: $ (645.9444)
MSFT: $ (514.129)
ORCL: $ (469.03384)
Producer sending price update(1)
AAPL: $ (163.04951)
GOOG: $ (560.21594)
```

And in the terminal window where you started the consumers, you should see that the consumer is receiving the stock price update events our producer is firing, but only the ones with the ticker symbol GOOG:

```
Starting example Stock Ticker Consumer now...
Price Update: GOOG[$330.88095]
Price Update: GOOG[$873.3398]
Price Update: GOOG[$423.3238]
Price Update: GOOG[$256.38521]
```

How it works...

There are times when you want the consumer messages from a topic or queue but you need only a subset of the messages that are being placed into the destination. An example of this would be an application that only wants to process orders for North America, or in the case of our sample application, we only want to read stock price updates for a specific company. To accomplish this we employ the **JMS selector** functionality in our topic subscription.

What is a JMS selector?

A selector is a way of attaching a filter to a given subscription, also known as **content-based routing**. In JMS, the selector uses message properties and headers compared against Boolean expressions to filter messages. The Boolean expressions are defined using SQL92 syntax. The following table summarizes the selector language used in JMS:

Element	Valid values
Identifiers	Property or header field reference (such as JMSCorrelationID, price, and date).
	The following values are not possible: NULL, TRUE, FALSE, NOT, AND, OR, BETWEEN, LIKE, IN, IS.
Operators	AND, OR, LIKE, BETWEEN, =, <>, <, >, <=, >=, IS NULL, IS NOT NULL.
Literals	The two Boolean literals, TRUE and FALSE.
	Exact number literals that have no decimal point; for example, +20 and -256, 42.
	Approximate number literals. These literals can use scientific notation or decimals; for example, -21.4E4, 5E2 and +34.4928.

Adding selectors to subscriptions

The code for the sample stock price consumer application in this recipe is identical to the consumer code from the previous recipe except for a few small changes. Let's take a look at the code and see how we apply a selector to our consumer's subscription:

```java
public class SelectiveTickerConsumer {

    private final String connectionUri = "tcp://localhost:61616";
    private ActiveMQConnectionFactory connectionFactory;
    private Connection connection;
    private Session session;
    private Destination destination;
    private String selector;

    public void before() throws Exception {
        connectionFactory = new
            ActiveMQConnectionFactory(connectionUri);
        connection = connectionFactory.createConnection();
        connection.start();
        session = connection.createSession(
            false, Session.AUTO_ACKNOWLEDGE);
        destination = session.createTopic("EVENTS.QUOTES");
        selector = System.getProperty(
            "QuoteSel", "symbol = 'GOOG'");
    }

    public void run() throws Exception {
        System.out.println(" Running example with selector: " +
selector);

        MessageConsumer consumer =
            session.createConsumer(destination, selector);
        consumer.setMessageListener(new EventListener());
        TimeUnit.MINUTES.sleep(5);
        connection.stop();
        consumer.close();
    }
}
```

As you can see in the sample code, we added a variable named `selector` to our consumer application and initialized it by reading a system property named `QuoteSel`, which defaults to `symbol = 'GOOG'`. We then pass in our set selector value to the `Session` object's `createConsumer()` method and that's it; the remainder of the code is unchanged.

By default our example stock price consumer will now only receive price updates for the ticker symbol `GOOG`. We can alter this by running the consumer application again and specifying a different selector and then running the price update producer application again. Try it yourself by running the demos again but using some different selector values.

To receive updates for both `GOOG` and `AAPL` run your consumer with:

```
$mvn exec:java –DQuoteSel="symbol='GOOG' OR symbol='AAPL'
```

To receiver updates for `MSFT` but only when the price is greater than $800 try:

```
$mvn exec:java –DquoteSel="symbol='MSFT' AND price >= 800"
```

Practice yourself by coming up with more selectors on your own and rerunning the consumer and producer applications.

There's more...

The JMS specification covers the various syntax rules governing its selector expression language quite well in the API documentation for the `Message` object; you can review the API documentation here: `http://docs.oracle.com/javaee/1.4/api/javax/jms/Message.html`.

Sparse matching selectors

ActiveMQ uses a paging architecture for messages that are stored on the broker. By default only a certain number of pages are brought into memory at any given time for a destination and this can have an impact on your consumers that use message selectors. If the destination contains a large number of messages and the selector doesn't match any of the messages that have been paged in, your consumer can stall until either the messages that are paged in are acknowledged or expired.

This sort of scenario happens most often when your selector is a **sparse matching selector** meaning it only matches a few messages out of the larger whole. If this happens, you can work around this issue by increasing the page size ActiveMQ uses for a destination. Refer to the documentation on setting destination policies for more information:

`http://activemq.apache.org/per-destination-policies.html`

Using the JMS request/response pattern (Intermediate)

In this recipe we are going to take a look at a messaging pattern known as request/response messaging.

Getting ready

We will use two examples for this recipe: **jms-requester** and **jms-responder**. Together they implement a simple request/response application.

How to do it...

To run the samples for this recipe, you will need to perform the following steps:

1. Open a terminal and start a broker.
2. Open a second terminal, change to the directory where the jms-responder example is located, and run it by typing `mvn compile exec:java`. (You can shut down the example by pressing *Ctrl + C* when done or allow it to stop on its own after five minutes.)
3. Open a third terminal, change to the directory where the jms-requester example is located, and run the example by typing `mvn compile exec:java`.

In the terminal where you started the jms-requester, you will see the following output indicating that the request application is sending request messages and receiving responses:

```
Starting Requester example now...
Job Request
Job Request
Job Finished
Job Request
Job Request
Job Finished
Job Request
Job Finished
Job Finished
Woohoo! Work's all done!
Finished running the Requester example.
```

And in the terminal window where you started the jms-responder example, you should see that the responder is receiving the request events from our requester example.

```
Starting Responder example now...
Job Request
Job Request
Job Request
Job Request
Job Request
Job Request
```

How it works...

While decoupling of messaging applications is a primary driver of the JMS specification, there are cases where an application needs to send a request and will not continue until it receives a response indicating its request was handled. This sort of messaging pattern is known as request/response messaging, and you can think of it as a sort of **Remote Procedure Call** (**RPC**) over JMS if that helps.

Traditionally, this type of architecture has been implemented using TCP client and server applications that operate synchronously across a network connection. There are several problems that arise in this implementation, the biggest of which can be scaling. Because the TCP client and server are tightly coupled, it's difficult to add new clients to handle an increasing workload. Using messaging based architecture we can reduce or eliminate this scaling issue along with other issues of fault tolerance and so on. In the messaging paradigm, a requester sends a request message to a queue located on a remote broker and one or more responders can take this message, process it, and return a response message to the requester. In the following diagram, we see a visual depiction of the typical implementation of the request/ response pattern over JMS:

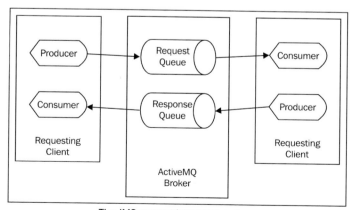

The JMS request/response pattern

As we can see in the previous diagram, each JMS request/response application follows a simple fixed pattern. But there are a lot of moving parts we need to understand. Let's now examine the source code for the examples we executed earlier and see how this messaging pattern is implemented in our JMS applications.

The JMS request application

Our simpler requester application places several requests onto a queue on our ActiveMQ Broker, and then it waits until all its outstanding requests are processed before finishing. Let's take a look at this in the following code:

```
public class RequesterExample implements MessageListener {

    private final String connectionUri = "tcp://localhost:61616";
    private ActiveMQConnectionFactory connectionFactory;
    private Connection connection;
    private Session session;
    private Destination destination;
    private static final int NUM_REQUESTS = 10;
    private final CountDownLatch done = new CountDownLatch(NUM_
REQUESTS);

    public void before() throws Exception {
        connectionFactory = new
            ActiveMQConnectionFactory(connectionUri);
        connection = connectionFactory.createConnection();
        connection.start();
        session = connection.createSession(
            false, Session.AUTO_ACKNOWLEDGE);
        destination = session.createQueue("REQUEST.QUEUE");
    }

    public void run() throws Exception {
        TemporaryQueue responseQ = session.createTemporaryQueue();
        MessageProducer requester =
            session.createProducer(destination);
        MessageConsumer responseListener =
            session.createConsumer(responseQ);
        responseListener.setMessageListener(this);

        for (int i = 0; i < NUM_REQUESTS; i++) {
            TextMessage request =
                session.createTextMessage("Job Request");
            request.setJMSReplyTo(responseQ);
            request.setJMSCorrelationID("request: " + i);
            requester.send(request);
        }
```

```
    if (done.await(10, TimeUnit.MINUTES)) {
        System.out.println("Woohoo! Work's all done!");
    }
    else {
        System.out.println("Doh!! Work didn't get done.");
    }
}

public void onMessage(Message message) {
    try {
        String jmsCorrelation = message.getJMSCorrelationID();
        if (!jmsCorrelation.startsWith("request")) {
            System.out.println("Received an unexpected response: " +
jmsCorrelation);
        }
        TextMessage txtResponse = (TextMessage) message;
        System.out.println(txtResponse.getText());
        done.countDown();
    }
    catch (Exception ex) {
    }
}
}
```

As you can see in the preceding code, the request application creates a JMS
`MessageProducer` object for sending its request along with a `MessageConsumer` object to
listen for the response. We've already seen code similar to this in other recipes; the question
here is about how we told the responder where to send its response.

The `JMSReplyTo` property for a JMS message was added just for this sort of messaging
pattern. The responder application doesn't have to know anything about preconfigured
destinations for sending responses, it just needs to query the message for its `JMSReplyTo`
address. This is yet another example of the benefits of the loose coupling that comes from
using the JMS API.

In our sample application, we create a JMS temporary queue and assign that to `JMSReplyTo`
for every request message we send. A JMS temporary destination works a lot like its non-
temporary counterpart, however there are three key differences:

▶ The lifetime of a temporary destination is tied to that of the connection object that
   created it. Once the connection is closed, the temporary destination is destroyed.

▶ Only a `MessageConsumer` object created from the connection that created the
   temporary destination can consume from that temporary destination.

▶ Temporary destinations don't offer the message persistence or reliability guarantees
   that normal destinations do.

Did you notice that we also assign a correlation ID to each request? Why do we do that? Since there could be multiple responses for requests we've sent, we might want to match up each response to ensure all our work gets done. For example, our application could have stored the correlation IDs in a map along with the job data and matched up the responses. Also, our application could have checked on a timeout if any outstanding requests hadn't arrived and could have resubmitted the unfinished job, or logged a warning to the administrator. The JMSCorrelationID field allows you to build this sort of book keeping into your request/response applications easily.

The JMS response application

In order to implement our simple responder application, we assemble many of the same JMS elements we did in the requester example; lets take a look at this in the following code:

```
public class ResponderExample implements MessageListener {

    private final String connectionUri = "tcp://localhost:61616";
    private ActiveMQConnectionFactory connectionFactory;
    private Connection connection;
    private Session session;
    private Destination destination;
    private MessageConsumer requestListener;
    private MessageProducer responder;

    public void before() throws Exception {
        connectionFactory = new
            ActiveMQConnectionFactory(connectionUri);
        connection = connectionFactory.createConnection();
        connection.start();
        session = connection.createSession(
            false, Session.AUTO_ACKNOWLEDGE);
        destination = session.createQueue("REQUEST.QUEUE");
        responder = session.createProducer(null);
        requestListener = session.createConsumer(destination);
        requestListener.setMessageListener(this);
    }

    public void run() throws Exception {
        TimeUnit.MINUTES.sleep(5);
    }

    public void onMessage(Message message) {
        try {
```

```
        Destination replyTo = message.getJMSReplyTo();
        if (replyTo != null) {
            TextMessage textMessage = (TextMessage) message;
            System.out.println(textMessage.getText());
            Message response =
                session.createTextMessage("Job Finished");
            response.setJMSCorrelationID(
                message.getJMSCorrelationID());
            responder.send(replyTo, response);
        }
    }
    catch (Exception e) {
        System.out.println(
            "Encounted an error while responding: " +
            e.getMessage());
    }
  }
}
```

As you can see, we create both a producer and consumer for our response example once again; however, we did something a bit different here. Did you spot it? The MessageProducer object we created was assigned a null destination; this is called an anonymous producer. We can use the anonymous producer to send messages to any destination, which is great since we don't know at startup which destination we are going to publish our responses to. We'd rather not create a new MessageProducer object every time a message arrives since that would add more network traffic and load to our broker.

When a request message is received by the responder application, it queries the message for the JMSReplyTo destination to which it should send the response. Once the responder knows where to send its answer, it constructs the appropriate response message and assigns it the JMSCorrelationID method that the requester will use to identify the response prior to sending it back to the responder.

Now we can start to imagine how our request/response applications can scale as the number of responders can grow with the increasing workload. If we need a new responder, we can spin up another instance on a different machine; it will share the load with all the others by taking one request at a time off the shared request queue and eventually sending its response back when its done. If, for instance, each request takes about a minute to complete, our sample would finish in about ten minutes. But if we add another responder application, we can cut that time in half.

There's more...

Every JMS request/response application we develop follows the basic pattern we saw in this recipe. Looking at the code, we start to see how JMS code can become a bit tedious with all the setup of connections, sessions, producers and consumers. Fortunately, there are ways to reduce the amount of work needed by using other software components that exist on top of the JMS API and provide simpler abstractions to problems such as the request/response pattern. One such solution is the Apache Camel project (http://camel.apache.org/). Apache Camel is what's known as an integration framework that implements well-known **Enterprise Integration Patterns** (**EIPs**) such as request/response.

Not only do Camel as well as other EIP frameworks provide a simpler way of implementing patterns such as request/response, they also build in error handling and recovery mechanics that make the developer's life simpler. It's a good idea to explore an EIP framework when you need to implement the more complex messaging patterns.

Some things to remember about temporary destinations

In an application that does a lot of request/response messaging, using temporary destinations for each response can create a large build up of resource utilization on the ActiveMQ Broker. Remember that temporary destinations don't go away until the connection that created them does. So, for a long running application that uses a connection, those destination resources created by the connection would never be recovered. In ActiveMQ, it's possible to configure a periodic cleanup of older inactive destinations to recover otherwise wasted resources. The documentation for this feature can be found at: http://activemq. apache.org/delete-inactive-destinations.html

Scheduling message delivery (Advanced)

In this recipe we will learn how to schedule message delivery in ActiveMQ.

Getting ready

For this recipe, we will use the example code in the message-scheduling project to show how you can schedule a message for later delivery. The default ActiveMQ configuration file doesn't turn on the message scheduler service. So, you will need to edit the activemq.xml file in the conf directory where you installed your broker and add the schedulerSupport="true" value to the broker XML tag, it should look something like this:

```
<broker xmlns="http://activemq.apache.org/schema/core"
brokerName="localhost" dataDirectory="${activemq.data}"
schedulerSupport="true">
```

How to do it...

To run the sample for this recipe, you will need to perform the following steps:

1. Open a terminal and start a broker.
2. Open a second terminal, change to the directory where the `message-scheduling` example is located, and run it by typing `mvn compile exec:java`.

In the terminal where you started the scheduling example, you will see output like the following, indicating that the application has scheduled a message. After a few seconds, the broker will begin to send the scheduled message back to the application.

```
Starting Scheduled Message example now...
Wakeup call set, going to sleep now.
Wake Up!
Wake Up!
Wake Up!
Wake Up!
Wake Up!
Wake Up!
Wake Up!
Wake Up!
Wake Up!
Wake Up!
Fine! I'm awake!
Finished running the Scheduled Message example.
```

How it works...

Scheduling a message in ActiveMQ is quite simple. There are no new JMS APIs to learn, and everything is done using the tools we've already learned in the previous recipes in this book. Let's first take a look at the code for the example we just executed, and then we'll walk through how it works:

```java
public class MessageSchedulingExample implements MessageListener {

    private final String connectionUri = "tcp://localhost:61616";
    private ActiveMQConnectionFactory connectionFactory;
    private Connection connection;
    private Session session;
```

```
private Destination destination;
private MessageProducer producer;
private MessageConsumer consumer;

private final long delay = TimeUnit.SECONDS.toMillis(10);
private final long period = TimeUnit.SECONDS.toMillis(5);
private final int repeat = 9;

private final CountDownLatch done = new CountDownLatch(10);

public void before() throws Exception {
  connectionFactory = new
      ActiveMQConnectionFactory(connectionUri);
  connection = connectionFactory.createConnection();
  session = connection.createSession(
      false, Session.AUTO_ACKNOWLEDGE);
  destination = session.createTopic("Alarm.Clock");
  producer = session.createProducer(destination);
  consumer = session.createConsumer(destination);
  consumer.setMessageListener(this);
  connection.start();
}

public void onMessage(Message message) {
  try {
      TextMessage text = (TextMessage) message;
      System.out.println(text.getText());
  }
  catch (JMSException e) {
  }
  done.countDown();
}

public void run() throws Exception {
  TextMessage message = session.createTextMessage("Wake Up!");
  message.setLongProperty(
      ScheduledMessage.AMQ_SCHEDULED_DELAY, delay);
  message.setLongProperty(
      ScheduledMessage.AMQ_SCHEDULED_PERIOD, period);
  message.setIntProperty(
      ScheduledMessage.AMQ_SCHEDULED_REPEAT, repeat);
  producer.send(message);
  done.await(5, TimeUnit.MINUTES);
}
}
```

In this example, we want to schedule a type of wake-up-call message to be delivered after a 20 second delay and then have it delivered again every ten seconds, nine more times. To schedule the message for delivery, we simply create the message and add the appropriate headers to it that the broker will use to apply the schedule. The destination that we send the scheduled message to is the one that the broker will use to later deliver the message.

Our sample application uses the predefined message header values in the ScheduledMessage utility class provided in the ActiveMQ Client JAR; however, these are just string values, so you don't absolutely need to import that class into your code. The available header values for scheduled messages are shown in the following table:

Scheduler header	Meaning
AMQ_SCHEDULED_DELAY	The time in milliseconds that the broker will hold the message for before scheduling it for delivery.
AMQ_SCHEDULED_PERIOD	The time in milliseconds to wait between successive message deliveries.
AMQ_SCHEDULED_REPEAT	The number of times the message will be rescheduled for delivery after the first scheduled delivery is completed.
AMQ_SCHEDULED_CRON	Scheduled message delivery based on a standard CRON tab entry. This value always takes priority over the delay and repeat period.

The CRON-based scheduler field can be used to do more complicated scheduling than can be done with the other fields. Let's say you want to schedule a message for delivery once an hour; you can do so using code similar to the following:

```
MessageProducer producer = session.createProducer(destination);
TextMessage message = session.createTextMessage();
message.setStringProperty(ScheduledMessage.AMQ_SCHEDULED_CRON, "0 * *
* *");
producer.send(message);
```

We can get even more elaborate by combining the CRON settings and the other settings for delay repeat and period. The CRON entry takes precedence over the other values. For instance, if we have a message that should be delivered 10 times at the start of every hour and we wanted a 1 second delay between each message, we could do so using the following code:

```
MessageProducer producer = session.createProducer(destination);
TextMessage message = session.createTextMessage();
message.setStringProperty(
    ScheduledMessage.AMQ_SCHEDULED_CRON, "0 * * * *");
message.setLongProperty(
    ScheduledMessage.AMQ_SCHEDULED_DELAY, 1000);
message.setLongProperty(
```

```
    ScheduledMessage.AMQ_SCHEDULED_PERIOD, 1000);
message.setIntProperty(
    ScheduledMessage.AMQ_SCHEDULED_REPEAT, 9);
producer.send(message);
```

Scheduled messages can be useful in a number of different scenarios; here, we use the message as a trigger to shut down our sample application after a predefined number of messages have been received, but there are plenty of other uses for this functionality. Imagine, for instance, a scheduled message that fires once a day to trigger your application to do some cleanup job that purges daily logs or to trigger some other batch processing type jobs.

There's more...

It's great that we can schedule messages for later delivery, but what happens if we want to later cancel a scheduled message or find out what the current set of scheduled messages is? Fortunately, these sorts of management activities can easily be accomplished right in your Java code. You could also use some external tools, such as JMX or the ActiveMQ Broker's web console, but these are outside the scope of this book.

Managing scheduled messages on the broker generally consists of creating a standard `MessageConsumer` instance and sending a control message to a predefined topic destination on the broker named ActiveMQ.Scheduler.Management. For actions that require the broker to send back responses, we make use of the `JMSReplyTo` message property just as we did in the previous recipe that talked about request/response messaging. Let's take a look now at code that instructs the broker to send us all the currently scheduled messages:

```
Destination management = session.createTopic(ScheduledMessage.AMQ_
SCHEDULER_MANAGEMENT_DESTINATION);

Destination browseDest = session.createTemporaryQueue();
MessageConsumer browser = session.createConsumer(browseDest);

MessageProducer producer = session.createProducer(management);
Message request = session.createMessage();
request.setStringProperty(
    ScheduledMessage.AMQ_SCHEDULER_ACTION,
    ScheduledMessage.AMQ_SCHEDULER_ACTION_BROWSE);

request.setJMSReplyTo(browseDest);
producer.send(request);

Message scheduled = browser.receive(5000);
while (scheduled != null) {
    // Do something with Message...
}
```

As you can see from the code, the way we browse the scheduled message looks a lot like the request/response pattern. The message we send to the broker needs to indicate what action the message scheduler is being asked to perform; we do that by specifying the AMQ_ SCHEDULER_ACTION_BROWSE option for the AMQ_SCHEDULER_ACTION message header. The broker fires them all to our supplied JMSReplyTo destination, and we just use a normal MessageConsumer object to read them.

Now that we've seen how to browse the messages that are scheduled for delivery, let's take a look at how to manage the scheduled messages that you've browsed. Each scheduled Message that is sent to your consumer contains a Job ID that can be used to remove that message from the scheduler using the same management destination that you used to request the browse action, the following is an example of that:

```
Message remove = session.createMessage();
remove.setStringProperty(
    ScheduledMessage.AMQ_SCHEDULER_ACTION,
    ScheduledMessage.AMQ_SCHEDULER_ACTION_REMOVE);
remove.setStringProperty(ScheduledMessage.AMQ_SCHEDULED_ID,
                scheduled.getStringProperty(ScheduledMessage.AMQ_
SCHEDULED_ID));
producer.send(remove);
```

Here, we create a new message instance and set the scheduler action AMQ_SCHEDULER_ ACTION_REMOVE to indicate we are sending a remove request. Then, we tag the request with the Job ID for a scheduled message by querying the message for its AMQ_SCHEDULED_ID message property.

If we want to remove some scheduled messages but don't want to browse them, just to find the ones we're interested in, we can do so using the remove option we just saw. But, instead of specifying a Job ID, we can give the broker a time window in which to operate. The Following is an example that shows a remove operation requested for all scheduled messages in the next hour:

```
long start = System.currentTimeMillis();
long end = System.currentTimeMillis() +
            TimeUnit.HOURS.toMillis(1);

Destination management = session.createTopic(
    ScheduledMessage.AMQ_SCHEDULER_MANAGEMENT_DESTINATION);

MessageProducer producer = session.createProducer(management);
Message request = session.createMessage();
request.setStringProperty(
    ScheduledMessage.AMQ_SCHEDULER_ACTION,
    ScheduledMessage.AMQ_SCHEDULER_ACTION_REMOVEALL);
```

```
request.setStringProperty(
    ScheduledMessage.AMQ_SCHEDULER_ACTION_START_TIME,
    Long.toString(start));
request.setStringProperty(
    ScheduledMessage.AMQ_SCHEDULER_ACTION_END_TIME,
    Long.toString(end));

producer.send(request);
```

Lastly, we could just remove all scheduled messages from the broker if we needed to; we do this with a single message sent to the management destination with the scheduler action of `AMQ_SCHEDULER_ACTION_REMOVEALL` set.

```
Destination management = session.createTopic(
    ScheduledMessage.AMQ_SCHEDULER_MANAGEMENT_DESTINATION);

MessageProducer producer = session.createProducer(management);
Message request = session.createMessage();
request.setStringProperty(
    ScheduledMessage.AMQ_SCHEDULER_ACTION,
    ScheduledMessage.AMQ_SCHEDULER_ACTION_REMOVEALL);

producer.send(request);
```

As you can see, you don't absolutely need any external tools to manage the scheduled messages on the broker. You can implement management write in your application using standard JMS API calls.

Activity monitoring in ActiveMQ (Advanced)

In this recipe we will look at how you can monitor activity in ActiveMQ Broker using the JMS API and the broker's built-in **Advisory Message** feature. Advisory messages from the broker allow your application to monitor events on the broker such as:

- ▶ Connections, consumers, and producers starting and stopping
- ▶ Temporary destinations being created and destroyed
- ▶ Messages expiring on topics and queues

Getting ready

In this recipe we will use two examples. The first example is named advisory-generator, which will cause the broker to produce some advisory messages. The second one is named advisory-consumer, which demonstrates how we can implement those broker advisories.

How to do it...

To run the sample for this recipe you will need to perform the following steps:

1. Open a terminal and start a broker.

2. Open a second terminal, change the path to the directory where advisory-consumer is located, and run it by typing `mvn compile exec:java` (you can shut it down by pressing *Ctrl + C* when done or you can allow it to stop on its own after 10 minutes).

3. Open a third terminal and change the path to the directory where advisory-generator is located and run the example by typing `mvn compile exec:java` (the sample will shut down on its own after a few minutes).

On the terminal where you started the example named advisory-consumer, you will see output like the following, indicating that the application is receiving advisory messages from the broker:

```
Starting Advisory Consumer example now...
New Producer Advisory, Producer Count: 1
New Producer Advisory, Producer Count: 5
New Producer Advisory, Producer Count: 5
New Producer Advisory, Producer Count: 5

New Producer Advisory, Producer Count: 2
New Consumer Advisory, Consumer Count: 1
New Producer Advisory, Producer Count: 1
New Consumer Advisory, Consumer Count: 0
New Producer Advisory, Producer Count: 0
Finished running the Advisory Consumer example.
```

The advisory source application runs without generating much output as it's just used here to create some activity on the broker.

How it works...

ActiveMQ Broker generates advisory messages for a number of different events that occur on the broker. Your client applications can subscribe to special topics where the events are sent in order to monitor activity on the broker. The advisory messages are just simple JMS message objects that can have some message properties set to provide helpful event-related information.

Our advisory-consumer example listens for events (related to `MessageProducer` and `MessageConsumer`) being added and removed from the broker for a particular destination; in this example we are watching the queue named `MyQueue`. Let's take a look at the code for the sample application:

```java
public class AdvisoryConsumerApp implements MessageListener {

    private final String connectionUri = "tcp://localhost:61616";
    private ActiveMQConnectionFactory connectionFactory;
    private Connection connection;
    private Session session;
    private Destination destination;
    private MessageConsumer advisoryConsumer;
    private Destination monitored;

    public void before() throws Exception {
        connectionFactory = new ActiveMQConnectionFactory
        (connectionUri);
        connection = connectionFactory.createConnection();
        session = connection.createSession(false, Session.AUTO_
        ACKNOWLEDGE);
        monitored = session.createQueue("MyQueue");
        destination = session.createTopic(
            AdvisorySupport.getConsumerAdvisoryTopic(monitored).
            getPhysicalName() + "," +
            AdvisorySupport.getProducerAdvisoryTopic(monitored).
            getPhysicalName());
        advisoryConsumer = session.createConsumer(destination);
        advisoryConsumer.setMessageListener(this);
        connection.start();
    }

    public void onMessage(Message message) {
        try {
            Destination source = message.getJMSDestination();
            if (source.equals(AdvisorySupport.getConsumerAdvisoryTopic
            (monitored))) {
                int consumerCount = message.getIntProperty
                ("consumerCount");
                System.out.println("New Consumer Advisory,
                Consumer Count: " + consumerCount);
            } else if (source.equals(AdvisorySupport.getProducerAdviso
            ryTopic(monitored))) {
```

```
                    int producerCount = message.getIntProperty("producerC
ount");

                    System.out.println("New Producer Advisory, Producer
Count: " + producerCount);
                }
        } catch (JMSException e) {
        }
    }
}
```

In order to receive advisory messages from the broker, our sample application subscribes to two different topics on the broker. The topics subscribed to are those special advisory topics that were mentioned earlier, and the ActiveMQ client library provides a convenience class named `AdvisorySupport` for fetching the various advisory topics available.

We use another ActiveMQ feature in this example to save some typing by subscribing to two destinations with one consumer. The destination passed to the `createConsumer` method is referred to as **Composite Destination**, which simply means we concatenated two destination names with a comma. We can add even more destinations if we want to.

In our sample application's `onMessage` callback method, we determine which advisory message we are receiving by examining the `JMSDestination` message property. Once we know which advisory message we are dealing with, we can find the consumer and producer counts for our monitored destination by accessing the `consumerCount` property that the broker adds to the advisory message.

There's more...

Advisory messages are enabled by default on the broker, although only a subset of the complete set will be generated by default. The complete list of advisory messages can be found on the ActiveMQ website, `http://activemq.apache.org/advisory-message.html`, along with information on the specific properties and contents of each advisory message.

Having the advisory messages enabled does generate a small amount of overhead on the network though, so they can be disabled in the broker's XML configuration file. In order to turn off advisory messages, we will add the `advisorySupport="false"` option to the `broker` XML element in the configuration file. It will look something like this:

```
<broker advisorySupport="false">...
```

Advisory messages are required for dynamic network broker topologies as network connectors subscribe to advisory messages. In the absence of advisories, a network must be statically configured.

Application testing using embedded brokers (Advanced)

In this recipe we are going to look at how you embed an ActiveMQ Broker right into your own applications.

Getting ready

For this recipe we will use the example application named embedded-broker to demonstrate embedded ActiveMQ Brokers. Before proceeding, you should ensure that there are no other broker instances running on your computer.

How to do it...

To run the sample for this recipe, open a terminal, change the path to the directory where embedded-broker is located, and run it by typing `mvn compile exec:java`.

In the terminal where you started the example, you will see output similar to the following snippet indicating that the application is running:

```
Starting the Embedded Broker example now...

We sent a Message!

Finished running the Embedded Broker example.

...
```

How it works...

The output of the example in this recipe certainly doesn't look very impressive; what is impressive though is that we didn't have to run a separate broker in order for our example code to work. Because ActiveMQ is a pure Java application, it can easily be embedded into our messaging applications, which can be useful not only in our applications but also for testing application code in continuous integration suites.

In order to embed the broker into our sample application, we first had to add some additional dependencies to our Maven POM file. When embedding brokers, you need to include the following code in your POM file:

```
<dependency>
    <groupId>org.apache.activemq</groupId>
    <artifactId>activemq-broker</artifactId>
    <version>5.8.0</version>
</dependency>
```

```
<dependency>
   <groupId>org.apache.activemq</groupId>
   <artifactId>activemq-kahadb-store</artifactId>
   <version>5.8.0</version>
</dependency>
<dependency>
   <groupId>org.apache.activemq</groupId>
   <artifactId>activemq-spring</artifactId>
   <version>5.8.0</version>
</dependency>
```

These additional libraries bring in everything we need to run a standard broker instance inside our example. Let's look at what each brings to the project:

- `<activemq-broker>`: As you might have guessed, this is where the core of the ActiveMQ Broker implementation resides. This is required any time you want to embed a broker in your application.

- `<activemq-kahadb-store>`: This library is the home of the default persistence adapter in ActiveMQ. You need to bring this in to use any of the default configurations.

- `<activemq-spring>`: This library brings in the code necessary to create a broker instance from an XML configuration file, be it a pure Spring file or the XBean-based configuration files that ship with ActiveMQ. This could also be omitted if you create the broker using pure Java code; we'll look at that a bit later.

There are of course other dependencies that might need to be brought into your project depending on what broker features you use; these are just the top three. ActiveMQ does provide a single, all-encompassing library named `<activemq-all>` that can be included in your Maven POM file. This is useful but does mean your application will acquire a lot of extra dependencies that you will never actually use.

Our sample application consists of the code from our first recipe, *Installing ActiveMQ (Simple)*, modified to create a broker directly in the code. Let's take a look at the code:

```
public class EmbeddedSimpleJMS {

    private final String connectionUri = "tcp://localhost:61616";
    private ActiveMQConnectionFactory connectionFactory;
    private Connection connection;
    private Session session;
    private Destination destination;
    private BrokerService service;

    public void before() throws Exception {
```

```
        service =
          BrokerFactory.createBroker("xbean:activemq.xml");
        service.start();

        connectionFactory = new
          ActiveMQConnectionFactory(connectionUri);
        connection = connectionFactory.createConnection();
        connection.start();
        session = connection.createSession(false,
          Session.AUTO_ACKNOWLEDGE);
        destination = session.createQueue("MyQueue");
    }

    public void after() throws Exception {

        if (connection != null) {
            try {
                connection.close();
            } catch (Exception ex) {}
        }

        if (service != null) {
            try {
                service.stop();
            } catch (Exception ex) {}
        }
    }

    public void run() throws Exception {

        MessageProducer producer =
          session.createProducer(destination);
        try {
            TextMessage message = session.createTextMessage();
            message.setText("We sent a Message!");
            producer.send(message);
        } finally {
            producer.close();
        }

        MessageConsumer consumer =
          session.createConsumer(destination);
        try {
            TextMessage message = (TextMessage)
              consumer.receive();
        } finally {
            consumer.close();
        }
    }
}
```

In the application's `before()` method, we use the class `BrokerFactory` to create ActiveMQ's `BrokerService` object, which is really an ActiveMQ Broker. The `BrokerFactory` class allows us to pass a configuration file that should be used to configure the newly created broker; in our case, we added a very basic ActiveMQ XML configuration file to our Maven project's `src/man/resources` directory so that it would automatically be added to the classpath. When the application shuts down, it must stop its `BrokerService` object, which we do in the `after()` method after we close our connection.

As you can see, it's extremely simple to embed ActiveMQ right inside your application. In ActiveMQ, we make use of this feature to write all of the unit tests for the project; each test creates a broker in its setup code and then shuts it down after the test has run. This is something you can use in your own application tests to ensure your code is using a broker instance with the correct configuration and a known state, without having to use any external tools.

There's more...

Our simple sample application created a broker using the `BrokerFactory` class and a configuration file. If, however, we just want to create a simple `BrokerService` instance without the need for a configuration file or dependency on the Spring library, we can create one using pure Java. To do this, we just need to create an instance of `BrokerService` and configure it according to our project's needs. The Java code to create a broker equivalent to the one we created in our example would be:

```
BrokerService broker = new BrokerService();
broker.addConnector("tcp://localhost:61616");
broker.start();
```

Here, we instantiate a `BrokerService` instance and add the connector for the TCP-based transport that our client connects to; everything else we leave at the broker's defaults. We could, if we want to, go one step further and disable persistence so that our sample doesn't need to pull in the `<activemq-kahadb-strore>` library in our project POM. The code for that would be:

```
BrokerService broker = new BrokerService();
broker.addConnector("tcp://localhost:61616");
broker.setPersistent(false);
broker.start();
```

When using embedded ActiveMQ Brokers, people general try to look for a way to restart the broker. There is no restart method or other facility in the `BrokerService` class to do a safe restart, so users are often tempted to call `stop()` followed by a call to `start()` later on, but this won't work. The correct method of restarting a `BrokerService` instance is shown in the following code snippet:

```
broker.stop();
broker.waitUnitStopped();
```

```
broker = new BrokerService();
broker.addConnector("tcp://localhost:61616");
broker.start();
```

Where to find more about configuring embedded brokers

More information on the options available when using an embedded broker can be found on the ActiveMQ website, `http://activemq.apache.org/how-do-i-embed-a-broker-inside-a-connection.html`.

Using ActiveMQ connection pools (Advanced)

In this recipe we will take a look at ActiveMQ's connection pooling library and see how using it in your applications can increase performance and reduce the load placed on your broker.

Getting ready

For this recipe, we will use the example application named connection-pools to demonstrate the use of the ActiveMQ pooling library. Before proceeding, you should ensure that there are no other broker instances running on your computer since our example uses the embedded broker trick we learned previously.

How to do it...

To run the sample for this recipe, open a terminal, change the path to the directory where connection-pools is located, and run it by typing `mvn compile exec:java`.

In the terminal where you started the example, you will see output like the following, indicating that the application is running:

```
Starting Pooled Connection example now...
Non-Pooled test took: 13 seconds
Pooled test took: 2 seconds
Finished running the Pooled Connection example.
```

How it works...

While the JMS API is connection oriented, meaning that our JMS applications are intended to open a connection and keep it open for long periods of time, not all applications fit this model. This is even though they use JMS as their messaging framework. ActiveMQ provides a solution to this problem by supplying a connection pooling library that allows your code more flexibility when it comes to working with JMS connections.

The ActiveMQ pooling library provides a solution for three common pooling scenarios when using the JMS API:

- ► Pooling of `Connection` objects for applications that either need to share a single connection or a set of connections among code that would otherwise result in many connections being opened and closed over time.
- ► Pooling of `Session` objects for a single connection for an application that would otherwise create and destroy large numbers of sessions over time.
- ► Pooling of `MessageProducer` objects for applications that either need a large number of `MessageProducer` instances or that create and destroy many `MessageProducer` instances over time.

Before we can use the pooling library effectively, we need to understand how it works and what we need to configure to better suit our applications' needs. In the next figure, we see the basic structure of classes that make up the pooling library and how they interact with each other:

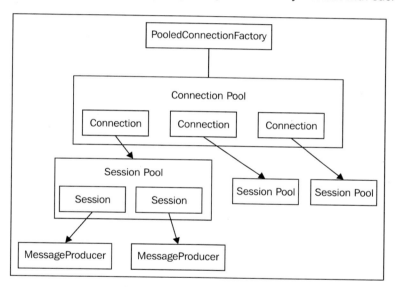

The first thing you should notice about the pooling library code is that it maintains the same structure as the standard ActiveMQ JMS client code. The code you write to use the pooling library is the standard JMS API code we've already learned to use; it's what's on the inside that counts. Let's examine each level of the library, and then we'll talk about how the example application for this recipe works.

The PooledConnectionFactory class

The `PooledConnectionFactory` class is our entry point into the pooling library; applications that use it generally create one `PooledConnectionFactory` instance and share it throughout the application code. `PooledConnectionFactory` exposes a number of configuration options to control how the `Connection` instances it creates behave. By default, `PooledConnectionFactory` creates a single `Connection` instance and returns that same instance every time the `createConnection()` methods are called.

Some applications, such as the example used in this recipe, can benefit from having more than one `Connection` instance in the pool, and it's easy enough to configure this using the factory's `setMaxConnections()` method. When the pool contains more than one connection, the connections are handed out in a round robin manner each time a create call is made; this provides a bit of load balancing across the connections for the resources created by each.

The PooledConnection class

Each time the `PooledConnectionFactory` instance is asked to create a connection it returns a `PooledConnection` instance that refers to one of the real connections in the pool. `PooledConnection` manages its own set of sessions in a session pool similar to the connection pool. Unlike the pooled connections, however, the sessions that are pooled in the connection are not shared; each call to create a session either returns a new session or a free one from the pool. The maximum number of sessions that `PooledConnection` will create is configurable, as is the behavior. When the maximum number has been reached, the code can either block any more sessions or it can throw an exception to indicate no more sessions can be created.

The PooledSession class

`PooledSession` also does its own sort of pooling for the `MessageProducer` objects it's asked to create. However, it is a bit different from the other object pools. Since a `MessageProducer` object can be created to be an anonymous producer and sent to any destination, the session creates a special wrapper that caches the destination your code asked it to associate with a JMS MessageProducer and always uses that cached destination to perform a send using a single `MessageProducer` instance, thereby saving the overhead of creating many different producer objects. While this still results in the allocation of objects on the client side, it saves the cost of the network overhead needed to register a new producer on the broker.

All of this may sound complicated but it's really not that bad. The classes in the pooling library behave pretty much the same as their pure JMS client counterparts. What you need to keep in mind is that when you close a `PooledSession` instance you close its cached producer, and when you close a `PooledConnection` instance you close all those `PooledSession` instances. The code that uses these types needs to ensure that it's taking advantage of the properties of the pooled library in a way that makes sense, otherwise it won't perform any better than the non-pooled JMS client code and could perform worse in some cases.

Our connection pooling example

The example application we ran earlier performed significantly better using the pooling library than it did using the plain ActiveMQ JMS client library code. Let's look at what the sample does and why it performs so much better.

The example application creates a `ThreadPoolExecutorService` instance that has a fixed thread pool of 10 and a `PooledConnectionFactory` instance which also sets its max connections to 10. The example then places 1,000 tasks into the executor; we show a portion of that code here:

```
connectionFactory = new ActiveMQConnectionFactory(connectionUri);
pooledFactory = new PooledConnectionFactory(connectionFactory);
...
ExecutorService service = Executors.newFixedThreadPool(10);

for (int i = 0; i < 1000; ++i) {
    service.execute(new Sender(factory.createConnection()));
}
```

As you can see, each of the queued tasks is given a connection from the `ConnectionFactory` instance we created. In the non-pooled case, we would be opening a large number of connections; this is not ideal as it involves a lot of network overhead adding each new connection to the broker. Each task in the executor then creates a session and sends some messages; let's take a look at that code now:

```
Session session = connection.createSession(false, Session.AUTO_
ACKNOWLEDGE);
for (int i = 0; i < 20; i++) {
    Destination destination = session.createTopic("TestTopic" + i);
    MessageProducer producer = session.createProducer(destination);
    producer.send(session.createMessage());
    producer.close();
}
```

As you can see, our task creates a session and then loops 20 times creating a `MessageProducer` instance each time in order to send to a specific destination on each send. In the non-pooled case, we'd be creating 20 `MessageProducer` objects in every loop and every task would create its own session. In the pooled case, though, we only create one session in each of the 10 connections and each session only creates one `MessageProducer` instance for each task as they are executed.

This example represents a worst-case scenario of bad JMS code that creates a lot of resources and destroys them without consideration for performance or resource utilization. It's because of this bad implementation that we see such a huge difference in performance between the pooled and non-pooled cases, but it makes clear the benefit of applying connection pooling in the right situations.

Once our example application finishes its work, it shuts down using the same style as our other examples by calling its `after()` method to clean up. Since we are using `PooledConnectionFactory` as opposed to the normal `ActiveMQConnectionFactory`, instance we need to ensure that those connections in the pool get shut down cleanly; we do that by calling the `clear()` method on `PooledConnectionFactory`; the code is shown here:

```
public void after() throws Exception {
    pooledFactory.clear();
    broker.stop();
}
```

Before we leave this section, it's good to note that we needed to update our standard Maven POM file for this project to make use of the ActiveMQ pooling library. We need to add one more dependency to our project. The XML is shown here:

```
<dependency>
  <groupId>org.apache.activemq</groupId>
  <artifactId>activemq-pool</artifactId>
  <version>5.8.0</version>
</dependency>
```

There's more...

You might have noticed that there was no mention of `MessageConsumer` objects being pooled by the ActiveMQ pooling library, and there's a good reason for that. Consumers, unlike connections, sessions, and `MessageProducer` resources, don't idle well. A `MessageConsumer` object continues to receive messages from ActiveMQ as long as its prefetch buffer is not full, and if it's sitting idle in a pool, those messages aren't being processed. And in the case of the queue, they aren't going to be sent to any other consumer until the `consumer` instance is closed. If we had several consumers sitting idle in our pool, they could collect a lot of messages that we might want to actually consume someplace else, causing our applications to behave in unexpected ways.

More information on configuring the pooling library

While the purpose of the pooling library is to keep our JMS resources open even when not being used, each of these resources does represent some overhead both on the client side and on the broker. We can configure our `PooledConnectionFactory` instance with an eviction time so that it will periodically close any resources that have sat idle in the pool for too long. Refer to the ActiveMQ API documentation at `http://activemq.apache.org/maven/5.8.0/apidocs/org/apache/activemq/pool/PooledConnectionFactory.html` for the various settings available for tuning `PooledConnectionFactory`.

Using Virtual Destinations (Advanced)

In this recipe we are going to look at ActiveMQ's **Virtual Destinations** feature and learn how it can save us from the many limitations that come with using durable topic subscriptions.

Getting ready

For this recipe we will use the sample application virtual-destinations to demonstrate the use of Virtual Destinations.

How to do it...

To run the sample for this recipe, open a terminal, change the path to point to the directory where virtual-destinations is located, and run it by typing `mvn compile exec:java`.

In the terminal where you started the example, you will see output similar to the following snippet, indicating that the application is running:

```
Starting Virtual Destination example now...
Queue A Consumer 1 processed 500 Messages
Queue A Consumer 2 processed 500 Messages
Queue B Consumer processed 1000 Messages
Finished running the Virtual Destination example.
```

How it works...

Our example takes advantage of ActiveMQ's Virtual Destination feature to allow a JMS Producer to send messages to a topic and have those messages be received by a number of queue consumers. Let's take a look at the sent code first:

```java
private void sendMessages() throws Exception {
    Connection connection =
      connectionFactory.createConnection();
    Session session = connection.createSession(false,
      Session.AUTO_ACKNOWLEDGE);
    Destination destination =
      session.createTopic("VirtualTopic.Foo");
    MessageProducer producer =
      session.createProducer(destination);
    for (int i = 0; i < 1000; ++i) {
        producer.send(session.createMessage());
    }
    connection.close();
}
```

As we can see, there's not much new here; we are just using standard JMS API code to send our messages. The important part is in the name of the topic destination `VirtualTopic.Foo`, which informs ActiveMQ Broker we want this topic to be one of those special Virtual Destinations.

Now let's take a look at the consumer code, and then we'll try and make sense of how this works:

```
Queue queueA =
    receiverSession.createQueue("Consumer.A.
    VirtualTopic.Foo");
VirtualMessageListener listenerA1 = new
    VirtualMessageListener(done);
MessageConsumer consumerA1 =
    receiverSession.createConsumer(queueA);
consumerA1.setMessageListener(listenerA1);
VirtualMessageListener listenerA2 = new
    VirtualMessageListener(done);
MessageConsumer consumerA2 =
    receiverSession.createConsumer(queueA);
consumerA2.setMessageListener(listenerA2);

Queue queueB =
    receiverSession.createQueue("Consumer.B.
        VirtualTopic.Foo");
VirtualMessageListener listenerB = new
    VirtualMessageListener(done);
MessageConsumer consumerB =
    receiverSession.createConsumer(queueB);
consumerB.setMessageListener(listenerB);
```

As we can see, the consumer code is also not very mysterious; we create two consumers on the `Consumer.A.VirtualTopic.Foo` queue and one on the `Consumer.B.VirtualTopic.Foo` queue, and yet when we run the example, the two consumers on queue A split 500 of the topic message and the consumer on queue B gets its own copy of the 1,000 messages. So what's happening on the broker then to make this happen?

By default, whenever a topic is created with a name matching the pattern `VirtualTopic.<TopicName>`, we gain access to the feature known as Virtual Destinations. These Virtual Destinations allow us to send a message to a topic but create consumers that have all the benefits of queue consumers, namely, those of load balancing and message persistence. Our queue consumers just need to use their own naming convention to access the Virtual Destination functionality. Each queue that we want to create must be named using the pattern `Consumer.<Name>.VirtualTopic.<TopicName>`.

In the following figure we can see a visual representation of the message flow in our example:

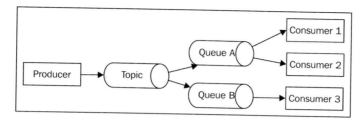

As messages are sent to our example's topic, they are distributed to both the queues we created. Two of our consumers split the work of processing messages from queue A, while the other consumer gets all the messages from queue B. In our example we didn't attach a listener to the topic itself, but we could have done so and it would also have received all the messages we sent. It's easy to imagine using the topic as a way to monitor the messages that are being distributed to the queue consumers in this scenario; this pattern is often referred to as a **wiretap**.

If it isn't already apparent, Virtual Destinations are a very powerful feature for your messaging applications. Topics are great for broadcasting events but when we need to be able to consume messages that were sent while a client was offline, the only recourse is to use a durable topic subscription. Unfortunately, durable subscriptions have a number of limitations, the least of which is that only one JMS connection can be actively subscribed to a logical topic subscription. This means that we can't load balance messages and we can't have fast failover if a subscriber goes down. Virtual Destinations solve these problems since all of our consumers subscribe to a queue so their messages are persistent, and the work of processing the messages on the queue can be shared by more than one active subscription.

There's more...

The naming pattern for Virtual Destinations is not set in stone. By default, ActiveMQ is configured to use the pattern we used in our sample application, but you can easily change this. In the following XML snippet, we configured our broker to all topics on our broker into virtual topics. We use the wildcard syntax here, which matches every topic name a client sends messages to:

```
<broker>
  <destinationInterceptors>
    <virtualDestinationInterceptor>
      <virtualDestinations><virtualTopic name=">" prefix="VirtualTopic
Consumers.*."/>
    </virtualDestinations></virtualDestinationInterceptor>
  </destinationInterceptors>
</broker>
```

More information on Virtual Destinations can be found on the ActiveMQ website, http://activemq.apache.org/virtual-destinations.html.

Using Failover transport (Advanced)

In this recipe we look at how we can create more robust JMS applications by making use of ActiveMQ's **Failover transport** to automatically reconnect a client to a broker in case of a connection failure. We will also discuss some general error-handling tips when using JMS in our applications.

Getting ready

For this recipe we will use two examples; the first is failover-producer and the second is failover-consumer that demonstrate how a lost connection doesn't have to affect our client applications.

How to do it...

To run the sample for this recipe, you will need to perform the following steps:

1. Open a terminal and start a broker.

2. Open a second terminal, change the path to the directory where failover-consumer is located, and run it by typing `mvn compile exec:java`.

3. Open a third terminal and change the path to point to the directory where failover-producer is located and run it by typing `mvn compile exec:java`.

4. While the producer and consumer applications are running, shut down the running broker instance and restart it.

In the terminal where you started the consumer example, you will see output similar to the following snippet, indicating that the application is running:

```
Starting example Failover Consumer now...
Failover Consumer received Message #1
Failover Consumer received Message #2
Failover Consumer received Message #3
Failover Consumer received Message #4
Failover Consumer received Message #5
Failover Consumer received Message #6
2013-03-06 14:15:23,731 [0.1:61616@59602] - WARN  FailoverTransport
- Transport (tcp://127.0.0.1:61616) failed, reason:  java.
io.EOFException, attempting to automatically reconnect
Failover Consumer received Message #7
Failover Consumer received Message #8
```

In the terminal windows where you started the producer example you will see output like following indicating that the application is running.

```
Starting example Failover Producer now...
Failover Producer sent Message #1
Failover Producer sent Message #2
Failover Producer sent Message #3
Failover Producer sent Message #4
Failover Producer sent Message #5
Failover Producer sent Message #6
2013-03-06 14:15:23,733 [0.1:61616@59606] - WARN  FailoverTransport
- Transport (tcp://127.0.0.1:61616) failed, reason:  java.
io.EOFException, attempting to automatically reconnect
Failover Producer sent Message #7
```

You can start and stop the broker as many times as you wish during the run of the examples; they will each detect and recover from the connection loss. The producer will finish after it has sent 1000 messages successfully to the queue.

How it works...

Up to this point in the book, we haven't really talked much about what happens when a broker fails while a client is producing or consuming messages. JMS, on its own, doesn't specify any sort of failover or loss of connection-handling behavior for the JMS provider. If your client connects to ActiveMQ Broker using the standard TCP-based transport protocol we've been using in our examples so far, when the broker fails, the client connection breaks and an exception will be generated as soon as the client notices that the connection is gone.

There are two ways your client can get notified of a connection error. The first is by an exception being thrown from a method call such as a `send()` operation, and the second is from an asynchronous exception listener registered on the `Connection` object. The asynchronous exception interface is shown here:

```
class ExceptionListener {
    void onException(JMSException ex);
}
```

In order to receive the asynchronous exceptions, your code implements the `ExceptionListener` interface and does something to react to the error. Reacting to the error is where things get complicated. There are a number of exception types defined in the JMS API. In spite of this, when an error occurs but your connection is still usable, it's tricky to tell whether you need to shut everything down and rebuild the JMS resources from scratch. Doing so is usually not a trivial bit of work inside your application. Fortunately, ActiveMQ provides us with an elegant solution to dealing with connection failures in our client applications.

ActiveMQ provides a Transport protocol known as Failover transport that can do the work of dealing with connection problems in our applications, leaving us to focus on our business logic and not worry about how we deal with every failure case. We used Failover transport in the examples for the recipe so that you could start and stop your broker as much as you wanted without the examples failing before they had sent and received all their messages.

Using Failover transport in our examples, or any of the other examples in this book, requires only one change to the way we we've implemented our code so far. That change is in the connection URI we passed to our `ConnectionFactory` instance; here's what the URI looks like in this recipe's examples:

```
failover:tcp://localhost:61616
```

That's it, we just added one little word, "failover", to the connection URI and the client becomes fault tolerant. That's pretty great right?

Failover transport isn't limited to just keeping our client connected to only one broker. We can specify the address of several brokers on our client's connection URI and Failover transport will work its way through them as brokers fail, allowing us to ensure that our client can quickly recover when it loses contact with the connected broker. If we knew that there were two brokers on our network and we wanted our client to failover to another when needed, we could use a URI similar to the following one:

```
failover:(tcp://host1:61616,tcp://host2:61616)
```

You can add an entry for every broker on your network in this manner, and the client will connect to the next available broker whenever one goes down. By default, the transport selects a random host from the set of available hosts each time it tries to connect. You can alter the URI to make this process non-random with the following change.

```
failover:(tcp://host1:61616,tcp://host2:61616)?randomize=false
```

There's more...

When a client's connection is down and Failover transport is working to reconnect to another broker, any call that your client makes that involves sending information to the broker will be blocked until the connection is restored. It's possible to monitor what Failover transport is doing in your application by using the `TransportListener` interface provided by the ActiveMQ client API.

The `TransportListener` interface provides methods for being notified of connection interruption as well as resumption of connection. You can also listen in on the exceptions that are thrown and other commands sent from the broker. You create and add a `TransportListener` interface to your connection with the following code:

```
Class MyTransportListener implements TransportListener {
    public void onCommand(Object command) {}
```

```
    public void onException(IOException error) {

    public void transportInterupted() {
        // app logic
    }

    public void transportResumed() {
        // app logic
    }
}


MyTransportListener listener = new MyTransportListener();
((ActiveMQConnection) connection).addTransportListener(listener);
```

Implementing a `TransportListener` interface is a good way to add logging to your application that reports on the connection state of your client as well as logging exceptions.

Using Failover transport in a broker cluster

We said earlier that when you configure your client connection URI for failover, you can specify the address of several different brokers that the client can try connecting to when things go wrong. This is a great feature, but imagine that your client operates in a large cluster of ActiveMQ Brokers where broker instances can be added or removed at any time. It would be quite cumbersome to stop all the running clients, update their connection URIs, and restart them every time the broker cluster changes. Fortunately, there's a solution for this problem.

By enabling the update cluster clients option in your ActiveMQ Broker-side configuration file, you can have the broker send information to the clients that keeps their Failover transports updated on the brokers currently running in a cluster. Enabling this feature is simple; you just update your configuration to look like the following snippet:

```
<broker>
  ...
  <transportConnectors>
    <transportConnector name="openwire" uri="tcp://0.0.0.0:61616"
updateClusterClients="true" updateClusterFilter="*A*,*B*" />
  </<transportConnectors>
  ...
</broker>
```

Now, in your client code, you only need to specify the address of the first broker in your cluster and the client will be updated as other brokers are added.

It's also possible to have the brokers in a cluster rebalance the connected clients to more evenly distribute the load across the cluster using this update cluster clients feature. You can read more about this as well as other options available for configuring your failover-enabled clients on the ActiveMQ site, `http://activemq.apache.org/failover-transport-reference.html`.

Complete Failover transport configuration reference

Failover transport has a number of configuration options that allow your application to specify exactly how it wants the transport to behave. For instance, you can specify that the transport only attempts to connect to the broker a set number of times before giving up. The complete reference for Failover transport options can be found on the ActiveMQ website, `http://activemq.apache.org/failover-transport-reference.html`.

 **Thank you for buying**
Instant Apache ActiveMQ Messaging
Application Development How-to

About Packt Publishing

Packt, pronounced 'packed', published its first book *"Mastering phpMyAdmin for Effective MySQL Management"* in April 2004 and subsequently continued to specialize in publishing highly focused books on specific technologies and solutions.

Our books and publications share the experiences of your fellow IT professionals in adapting and customizing today's systems, applications, and frameworks. Our solution based books give you the knowledge and power to customize the software and technologies you're using to get the job done. Packt books are more specific and less general than the IT books you have seen in the past. Our unique business model allows us to bring you more focused information, giving you more of what you need to know, and less of what you don't.

Packt is a modern, yet unique publishing company, which focuses on producing quality, cutting-edge books for communities of developers, administrators, and newbies alike. For more information, please visit our website: www.packtpub.com.

Writing for Packt

We welcome all inquiries from people who are interested in authoring. Book proposals should be sent to author@packtpub.com. If your book idea is still at an early stage and you would like to discuss it first before writing a formal book proposal, contact us; one of our commissioning editors will get in touch with you.

We're not just looking for published authors; if you have strong technical skills but no writing experience, our experienced editors can help you develop a writing career, or simply get some additional reward for your expertise.

ZeroMQ

ISBN: 978-1-78216-104-2   Paperback: 108 pages

Use ZeroMQ and learn how to apply different message patterns

1. Learn fundamental message/queue design patterns

2. Work with multi-threaded programs

3. Work with multiple sockets

Instant Apache ServiceMix How-to

ISBN: 978-1-84951-966-3   Paperback: 292 pages

Learn to create simple ServiceMix-based integration solutions using short, practical, hands-on recipes

1. Learn something new in an Instant! A short, fast, focused guide delivering immediate results.

2. Leverage OSGI to speed up the ESB deployment

3. Define message flow with Camel DSL

4. Expose your system via web services

Please check **www.PacktPub.com** for information on our titles